T0318850

HYSTERIA FROM FREUD TO LACAN

THE LACANIAN CLINICAL FIELD

A series of books edited by
Judith Feher-Gurewich
in collaboration with Susan Fairfield

HYSTERIA FROM FREUD TO LACAN: THE SPLENDID CHILD OF PSYCHOANALYSIS

Juan-David Nasio

TRANSLATED AND EDITED BY
Susan Fairfield

OTHER

The Other Press, Llc
New York

This work, published as part of the program of aid for publication, received support from the Ministry of Foreign Affairs of the Cultural Service of the French Embassy in the United States. *Cet ouvrage publié dans le cadre du programme d'aide à la publication bénéficie du soutien du Ministère des Affaires Etrangères du Service Culturel de l'Ambassade de France représenté aux Etats-Unis.*

This book was set in 11 pt. Berkeley by Alpha Graphics of Pittsfield, New Hampshire.

ISBN   978-1-59051-602-3

Printed in the United States of America on acid-free paper. For information write to Other Press, LLC, 2 Park Avenue, 24th Floor, New York, NY 10016. Or visit our Web site: www.otherpress.com.

Library of Congress Cataloging-in-Publication Data

Nasio, Juan-David.
    [Hysterie. English]
    Hysteria from Freud to Lacan: the splendid child of
psychoanalysis / Juan-David Nasio; translated and edited by Susan
Fairfield.
      p. cm.—(The Lacanian clinical field)
    Previously published as Hysteria. Northvale, N.J.: J. Aronson,
© 1997.
    Includes bibliographical references and index.
    ISBN   1-892746-02-6
    1. Hysteria.   2. Psychoanalysis.   I. Fairfield, Susan.
II. Title.   III. Series.
    [RC532.N3513   1998]
    616.85'24—dc21   98-39631

To the memory of my father

the doctor. His work as clinician and researcher

was permeated by the desire

to understand the enigma of the body

that speaks the truth

of what we are.

Contents

The Lacanian Clinical Field:
Series Overview

Lacanian psychoanalysis exists, and the new series, The Lacanian Clinical Field, is here to prove it. The clinical expertise of French practitioners deeply influenced by the thought of Jacques Lacan has finally found a publishing home in the United States. Books that have been acclaimed in France, Italy, Spain, Greece, South America, and Japan for their clarity, didactic power, and clinical relevance will now be at the disposal of the American psychotherapeutic and academic communities. These books cover a range of topics, including theoretical introductions; clinical approaches to neurosis, perversion, and psychosis; child psychoanalysis; conceptualizations of femininity; psychoanalytic readings of American literature; and more. Thus far nine books are in preparation.

Though all these works are clinically relevant, they will also be of great interest to those American scholars who have taught and used Lacan's theories for over a decade. What better opportunity for the academic world of literary criticism, philosophy, human sciences, women's studies, film studies, and multicultural studies finally to have access to the clinical insights of a theorist known primarily for his revolutionary vision of the formation of the human subject. Thus The Lacanian Clinical Field goes beyond introducing the American clinician to a different psychoanalytic outlook. It brings together two communities that have grown progressively estranged from each other. For indeed, the time when the Frankfurt School, Lionel Trilling, Erich Fromm, Herbert Marcuse, Philip Rieff, and others were fostering exchanges between the academic and the psychoanalytic communities is gone, and in the process psychoanalysis has lost some of its vibrancy.

The very limited success of ego psychology in bringing psychoanalysis into the domain of science has left psychoanalysis in need of a metapsychology that is able not only to withstand the pernicious challenges of psychopharmacology and psychiatry but also to accommodate the findings of cognitive and developmental psychology. Infant research has put many of Freud's insights into question, and the attempts to replace a one-body psychology with a more interpersonal or intersubjective approach have led to dissension within the psychoanalytic community. Many theorists are of the opinion that the road toward scientific legitimacy requires a certain allegiance with Freud's detractors, who are convinced that the unconscious and its sexual underpinnings are merely an aberration. Psychoanalysis continues to be practiced, however, and according to both patients and analysts the uncovering of unconscious motivations continues to provide a sense of relief. But while there has been a burgeoning of different psychoanalytic schools of thought since the desacralization of Freud, no theoretical agreement has been reached as to why such relief occurs.

Nowadays it can sometimes seem that Freud is read much more scrupulously by literary critics and social scientists than by psychoanalysts. This is not entirely a coincidence. While the psychoanalytic community is searching for a new metapsychology, the human sciences have acquired a level of theoretical sophistication and complexity that has enabled them to read Freud under a new lens. Structural linguistics and structural anthropology have transformed conventional appraisals of human subjectivity and have given Freud's unconscious a new status. Lacan's teachings, along with the works of Foucault and Derrida, have been largely responsible for the explosion of new ideas that have enhanced the interdisciplinary movement pervasive in academia today.

The downside of this remarkable intellectual revolution, as far as psychoanalysis is concerned, is the fact that Lacan's contribution has been derailed from its original trajectory. No longer perceived as a theory meant to enlighten the practice of psychoanalysis, his brilliant formulations have been both adapted and criticized so as to conform to the needs of purely intellectual endeavors far removed from clinical reality. This state of affairs is certainly in part responsible for Lacan's dismissal by the psychoanalytic community. Moreover, Lacan's "impossible" style has been seen as yet another proof of the culture of obscurantism that French intellectuals seem so fond of.

In this context the works included in The Lacanian Clinical Field should serve as an eye-opener at both ends of the spectrum. The authors in the series are primarily clinicans eager to offer to professionals in psychoanalysis, psychiatry, psychology, and other mental-health disciplines a clear and succinct didactic view of Lacan's work. Their goal is not so much to emphasize the radically new insights of the Lacanian theory of subjectivity and its place in the history of human sciences as it is to show how this difficult and complex body of ideas can enhance clinical work. Therefore, while the American clinician will be made aware that Lacanian psychoanalysis is not primarily a staple of literary criticism or philosophy but a praxis meant to cure patients of their psychic distress, the academic community will be exposed for the first time to a reading of Lacan that is in sharp contrast with the literature that has thus far informed them about his theory. In that sense Lacan's teachings return to the clinical reality to which they primarily belong.

Moreover, the clinical approach of the books in this series will shed a new light on the critical amendments that literary scholars and feminist theoreticians have brought to Lacan's conceptualization of subjectivity. While Lacan has been applauded for having offered an alternative to Freud's biological determinism, he has also been accused of nevertheless remaining phallocentric in his formulation of sexual difference. Yet this criticism, one that may be valid outside of the clinical reality—psychoanalysis is both an ingredient and an effect of culture—may not have the same relevance in the clinical context. For psychoanalysis as a praxis has a radically different function from the one it currently serves in academic discourse. In the latter, psychoanalysis is perceived both as an ideology fostering patriarchal beliefs and as a theoretical tool for constructing a vision of the subject no longer dependent on a phallocratic system. In the former, however, the issue of phallocracy loses its political impact. Psychoanalytic practice can only retroactively unravel the ways in which the patient's psychic life has been constituted, and in that sense it can only reveal the function the phallus plays in the psychic elaboration of sexual difference.

The Lacanian Clinical Field, therefore, aims to undo certain prejudices that have affected Lacan's reputation up to now in both the academic and the psychoanalytic communities. While these prejudices stem from rather different causes—Lacan is perceived as too patriarchal and reactionary in the one and too far removed from clinical reality in the other—they both seem to overlook the fact that the fifty years that cover the period of Lacan's teachings were mainly devoted to working and reworking the meaning and function of psychoanalysis, not necessarily as a science or even as a human science, but as a practice that can nonetheless rely on a solid and coherent metapsychology. This double debunking of received notions may not only enlarge the respective frames of reference of both the therapeutic and the academic communities; it may also allow them to find a common denominator in a metapsychology that has derived its "scientific" status from the unexpected realm of the humanities.

I would like to end this overview to the series as a whole with a word of warning and a word of reassurance. One of the great difficulties for an American analyst trying to figure out the Lacanian "genre" is the way these clinical theorists explain their theoretical point of view as if it were coming straight from Freud. Yet Lacan's Freud and the American Freud are far from being transparent to each other. Lacan dismantled the Freudian corpus and rebuilt it on entirely new foundations, so that the new edifice no longer resembled the old. At the same time he always downplayed, with a certain *coquetterie*, his position as a theory builder, because he was intent on proving that he had remained, despite all odds, true to Freud's deepest insights. Since Lacan was very insistent on keeping Freudian concepts as the raw material of his theory, Lacanian analysts of the second generation have followed in their master's footsteps and have continued to read Freud scrupulously in order to expand, with new insights, this large structure that had been laid out. Moreover, complicated historical circumstances have fostered their isolation, so that their acquaintance with recent psychoanalytic developments outside of France has been limited. Lacan's critical views on ego psychology and selected aspects of object relations

theory have continued to inform their vision of American psychoanalysis and have left them unaware that certain of their
misgivings about these schools of thought are shared by some
of their colleagues in the United States. This apparently undy-
ing allegiance to Freud, therefore, does not necessarily mean that
Lacanians have not moved beyond him, but rather that their
approach is different from that of their American counterparts.
While the latter often tend to situate their work as a reaction
to Freud, the Lacanian strategy always consists in rescuing
Freud's insights and resituating them in a context free of biological determinism.

Second, I want to repeat that the expository style of the
books of this series bears no resemblance to Lacan's own writings. Lacan felt that Freud's clarity and didactic talent had ultimately led to distortions and oversimplifications, so that his own
notoriously "impossible" style was meant to serve as a metaphor
for the difficulty of listening to the unconscious. Cracking his
difficult writings involves not only the intellectual effort of read-
ers but also their unconscious processes; comprehension will
dawn as reader-analysts recognize in their own work what was
expressed in sibylline fashion in the text. Some of Lacan's fol-
lowers continued this tradition, fearing that clear exposition
would leave no room for the active participation of the reader.
Others felt strongly that although Lacan's point was well taken
it was not necessary to prolong indefinitely an ideology of
obscurantism liable to fall into the same traps as the ones Lacan
was denouncing in the first place. Such a conviction was precisely
what made this series, The Lacanian Clinical Field, possible.

—Judith Feher Gurewich, Ph.D.

Foreword

Until fairly recently, the majority of psychoanalysts in the United States had little interest in Lacanian analysis and only scant knowledge of it. At any rate, their knowledge was really not sufficient either to accept or to reject Lacan's ideas intelligently. What little was known—and this was at second hand—rather repelled than attracted. Quite apart from Lacan's obscure language and what appeared to be highly abstract concepts with no empirical foundation, the rumors of allegedly erratic and arbitrary behavior on his part contributed to this aversion.

Even less is known among psychoanalysts in this country about the significant creative contributions of Lacan's inner circle of collaborators and students, clinicians who are currently expanding and shaping Lacanian psychoanalysis in Paris and putting their individual stamp on it. Having understood Lacan's ideas and his clinical approach directly and profoundly, they have contributed their own clinical experiences to buttress a modern Lacanian structure of theory and practice.

The greater expository clarity of these contemporary Lacan-ians, coupled with an increasing openness and receptivity among psychoanalysts in this country to new and unfamiliar ideas, makes the appearance of Juan-David Nasio's book timely and assures a wider readership for it than it would have attracted in the past. Dr. Nasio is prominent among the highly articulate younger Lacanians, and his *L'hystérie, ou l'enfant magnifique de la psychanalyse* (1990c) is here presented in a superb transla-tion by Susan Fairfield. Those who read this translation will no longer be able to say that they cannot grasp Lacan's ideas. Dr. Nasio sets them forth with clarity, simplicity, and seasoned pedagogy, making obscure Lacanian theories experience-near wherever this is possible. And where it is not, his knowledge of the intricacies of the theory permits him to formulate it in such a way that we can understand it, even when we cannot accept it or assimilate it to our own conceptual framework.

With Dr. Nasio's clear and concise formulations, it is now easier to detect those elements of Lacan's (and now Nasio's) ideas that are similar to, or compatible with, our own reading of Freud and with aspects of the various contemporary psychoanalytic approaches in this country. Once we have worked our way through this volume, we end up with a compelling desire to know more. Having grasped the fundamentals, we wish we had the opportunity to follow the analysis of one of Dr. Nasio's cases through some detailed vignettes, so that we could more clearly understand just exactly how he translates his theoretical ideas into clinical practice. What he says he does is quite illuminat-ing; what he could actually show with clinical examples would be more compelling.

Still, Dr. Nasio offers us a great deal in this slim, attractively issued volume. There is no need to summarize—let the reader experience the full impact of the text. But to highlight the special features of his contributions with some remarks about how to approach this book, a few preliminary words are in order.

A consummate teacher, Dr. Nasio presents his reading of Freud's first theory of hysteria (with trauma at its center), followed by the second theory (with unconscious fantasy at its center), as the foundation upon which he elaborates his own understanding of hysteria, obsessional and phobic phenomena, and neurosis in general. He interprets hysteria—the paradigmatic clinical problem of psychoanalysis, the one that gave rise to psychoanalytic theory—on the basis of a Lacanian reading of Freud. This enables the American reader to make an immediate comparison with his or her own reading of Freud in the light of the many advances in psychoanalysis over the last few decades. What Dr. Nasio is able to encompass in this relatively brief presentation, after having laid the groundwork in a discussion of the familiar clinical-theoretical issues of hysteria, is truly remarkable. His narrative is organized as a logical sequence of questions, a format that enhances our grasp of his ideas as he moves from the observable phenomena to the deeper layers of the dynamics and structure of the neuroses.

One caveat: the reader must occasionally be willing and able to get beyond the terminology in order to penetrate to the intended meaning. This is especially important in view of the fact that much of Lacanian theory is couched in the psychoeconomic idiom of libido theory, less frequently relied on nowadays in this country. Such an effort at understanding will amply reward the reader who ventures beyond some of the language to the essence of the propositions.

I can speak here from personal experience. I knew very little about Lacan and nothing about current Lacanian work in France until, as part of a group of American psychoanalysts, I met with a number of Lacanian psychoanalysts in Paris for a conference organized by Dr. Judith Feher Gurewich of Boston, a highly sophisticated bridge builder between the two groups.* It was not an easy dialogue for most of us, but both sides made the effort to listen and to absorb all that could be absorbed in one week-end. It was in this context that I first met Dr. Nasio. He worked hard at both communicating his own ideas and trying to under-stand ours, demonstrating that, after years of lack of interest in their counterparts' "strange" theories, American and Lacanian analysts could finally begin to be receptive to each other's work. In a few additional, private discussions outside the conference, I had the opportunity to benefit from Dr. Nasio's well-organized articulation of his concepts, which he worked out in all of their intricate details, eager to illustrate on the napkins at the lunch table points that still needed clarification. The reader who stud-ies this volume with the necessary openness will derive the same pleasure and profit.

—Paul H. Ornstein, M.D.

Translator's note: The proceedings of this 1994 conference have been published as *The Subject and the Self: Lacan and American Psychoanalysis*, edited by Judith Feher Gurewich and Michel Tort, in collaboration with Susan Fairfield.

Opening Remarks

"Where have they gone, the hysterics of the past, these marvelous women—the Anna O's, the Doras . . ." (Lacan 1977b, p. 64), all those women who provided the womb from which psychoanalysis was born? It is owing to their words that Freud, as he listened to them, discovered an entirely new kind of human relationship. But the hysteria of those early years did not only give birth to psychoanalysis; it left an indelible stamp on the theory and practice of the discipline today. For above and beyond the changes that have inevitably taken place, the thinking of analysts nowadays and the techniques they utilize continue to be closely connected to the treatment of hysterical suffering. Psychoanalysis and hysteria are so inextricably linked that the governing principle of analytic therapy is this: to treat and cure hysteria, we have to create another hysteria artificially. The psychoanalysis of any neurosis, when all is said and done, is just the artificial setting up of a hysterical neurosis and its final resolution. If, by the end of the analysis, we have overcome this new, artificial neurosis—one that was entirely created between patient and analyst—then at the same time we shall have resolved the neurosis that initially brought the patient into treatment.

So the hysterics of the past have lived on, and their suffering can be seen in different clinical guises today—less obtrusive, less spectacular guises, perhaps, than those encountered at the Salpêtrière. Yet while the hysterics at the end of the nineteenth century experienced a different kind of suffering from that of their counterparts today, the explanation offered by psychoanalysis for the cause of this suffering has hardly changed. Psychoanalytic theory has, to be sure, undergone remarkable alterations since its beginnings, but its conception of the origin of hysteria has remained essentially the same. What is that origin? What is the Freudian theory of the psychic causality of hysteria? Or, to put it more simply, how does someone become a hysteric? And how can we cure such a person? Those are the questions we shall be considering in this book.

The Face of Hysteria in Analysis

Before I reply to these opening questions, let me sketch the clinical picture of hysteria today. It appears before us in two distinct ways, depending on how we look at it. For we can view it descriptively, with regard to its observable symptoms, in which case hysteria presents as a defined clinical entity; or we can look at it in relational terms and in that way conceptualize hysteria as an unhealthy bond linking the hysteric to another person—in particular, with regard to treatment, to that other who is the psychoanalyst.

If we start by placing ourselves in the position of an outside observer, we recognize in hysteria a generally latent neurosis that, for the most part, emerges at the time of significant events or critical periods in the life of a subject, as for example in adolescence. This neurosis appears in the form of varied, often transient difficulties, of which the classic manifestations are somatic symptoms such as motor disturbances (muscular contractions, disorders of gait, paralysis of limbs, facial paralysis, etc.); disturbances of feeling (local pain, migraines, loss of sensation in a given part of the body, etc.); and sensory disturbances (blindness, deafness, muteness, etc.). We also encounter a set of more specific complaints, from insomnia and minor fainting to alterations in consciousness, memory, or intelligence (dissociation, amnesia, etc.), all the way to serious states of pseudo-coma. All of these manifestations that afflict the hysteric, and especially the somatic symptoms, are characterized by a radically distinctive sign: they are most often transitory, they reflect no organic cause, and, in their bodily localization, they follow no law of anatomy or physiology. We shall see further on how all these forms of somatic suffering depend instead on another anatomy, a highly fantasmatic one, that operates unbeknownst to the patient.

Another clinical feature of hysteria, one we shall be returning to quite often, also concerns the body, but the body understood as sexed. In effect, the body of the hysteric suffers from being divided into the genital part, surprisingly anesthetic and afflicted with strong sexual inhibitions (premature ejaculation, frigidity, impotence, sexual disgust, etc.), and all the remaining, non-genital part of the body that, paradoxically, appears very erotized and subject to ongoing sexual excitation.

*
*   *

Let us change position now and take up the relational perspective, the one adopted by the analyst engaged in the task of listening. His conception of hysteria has been formed not only through the teachings of psychoanalytic theory, but above all through the experience of transference with the so-called hysterical analysand and—this should be emphasized—with his patients in general. Yes, with all his patients, since all patients in analysis inevitably go through a phase of hystericization at the time when the transference neurosis sets in. What, exactly, have we learned from our patients about hysteria? This book is meant to be an extended response to that question, but for the moment let us stay with the issue of the way hysteria presents itself in analysis.

From our place in the transference we can observe three states, or rather three permanent and enduring positions, of the hysterical ego.* Beyond the multiplicity of events that follow one another in the course of an analysis, and beneath the words, affects, and silences, we recognize three distinctive ego states that, in themselves, sum up the specific manifestation of hysteria. In the first of these, a passive position as it were, the ego is constantly expecting to receive from the other not a fulfilling satisfaction, but, curiously, a frustrating non-response. This disappointed expectation, always hard for the psychoanalyst to handle, results in the perpetual dissatisfaction and discontent of which the neurotic so often complains. The first state is thus that of an *unsatisfied ego*. Another typically hysterical position discernible in analysis is also an ego state, but here it is an active state of a hystericizing ego, one that transforms the concrete reality of the analytic space into a fantasmatic reality of a sexual nature. I shall be discussing in more detail below what this trans-

---

Translator's note: The French translation of Freud's *das Ich* ("the I") is *le moi*, "the me," which is closer in tone to the original than the Latinate "ego." In its simplicity and experiential immediacy, *le moi* sometimes corresponds to what the Anglo-American psychoanalytic tradition calls "the self." I am following convention in translating it as "the ego" because, as Paul Ornstein notes in his Foreword, Dr. Nasio often retains Freud's dynamic and economic model of the mind.

formation is like, and how we are to understand its character-
ization as "sexual," but for the moment I shall just state that the
hysterical ego erotizes the scene of the treatment. The second
state, then, is that of a *hystericizing ego*. There is yet a third subjective position of the hysteric, characterized by the sadness of
the ego when it must finally confront the sole truth of its being:
not knowing whether it is a man or a woman. This third state is
that of a *sadness ego*. Let us take a brief look at each of these ego
states in turn.

THE UNSATISFIED EGO

For psychoanalysis, hysteria is not, as is usually believed, an illness affecting an individual, but rather the unhealthy state of a
human relationship that subjects one person to another. Hysteria
is, above all, the name we give to the tie and the bonds that the
neurotic weaves in his relation with others through his fantasies.
The hysteric, like any neurotic subject, unknowingly applies the
sick logic of his unconscious fantasy in his affective tie to the other.
In this fantasy, he plays the role of a wretched and forever unsatisfied victim. It is precisely this fantasmatic state of dissatisfaction that marks and dominates the whole life of the neurotic.

But why fantasize and experience dissatisfaction when,
theoretically, it is happiness and pleasure that we supposedly
hope to achieve? The reason is obvious. The hysteric is basically a fearful being who, in order to lessen his anxiety, has
found no recourse other than to sustain unremittingly, in his
fantasies and in his life, the painful state of dissatisfaction. As
long as I'm dissatisfied, he would say, I'll be safe from the danger that lies in wait for me. But what is this danger? What is it
that the hysteric dreads? There is only one basic danger that

threatens him, an absolute peril, pure, without image or figuration, sensed rather than defined, namely the danger of experiencing the satisfaction of utmost pleasure, a pleasure that, were he to experience it, would make him crazy, make him dissolve or disappear.

It is irrelevant whether he imagines this utmost pleasure as the pleasure of incest, as undergoing death, or as agonizing pain, or whether he imagines the risks of this danger as taking the form of madness, dissolution, or the annihilation of his being: the problem is to avoid at all costs any experience that would suggest, directly or indirectly, a state of complete and absolute fulfillment. Such a state, while in fact impossible, is nonetheless sensed by the hysteric as a danger that could be actualized, as the supreme danger of being, one day, seized by ecstasy and experiencing pleasure to the ultimate point of death. In sum, the hysteric's problem is first and foremost his fear, a profound and definitive fear, never felt but active on all levels of his being, a fear concentrated on a sole danger: the act of experiencing pleasure. Fear and the persistent refusal to experience pleasure are at the center of the psychic life of the hysterical neurotic.

Now, in order to remove this threat of an accursed and dreaded pleasure, the hysteric unconsciously invents a fantasy scenario designed to prove to himself and to the world that there is no pleasure except the kind that is unfulfilled. For how to sustain discontent, if not by creating the fantasy of a monster whom we call the other, now strong and all-powerful, now weak and ill, always immense, always disappointing our expectations? And so every exchange with the other inevitably leads to dissatisfaction. As a result, the daily reality of the neurotic is shaped by this fantasy, and those close to him, whether loved or hated, take on the role of the unsatisfying other for him.

The hysteric treats his fellow human being, loved or hated, and especially his partner the psychoanalyst, in the same manner as he treats the other of his fantasy. How does he go about it? He seeks—and always finds!—the points where the strong other exploits that strength in order to humiliate, and he finds the points where the weak other uses that weakness to arouse compassion. With very acute perception, the hysteric detects in others the sign of a humiliating strength that will make him unhappy, or a touching weakness that moves him to pity but that he can do nothing to remedy. In short, whether it is a question of power or of defect in the other, whether the other belongs to fantasy or to reality, the hysteric always insists on finding that discontent is his best guardian. The world of neurosis, inhabited by nightmares, obstacles, and conflicts, thus becomes the sole protective bulwark against the absolute peril of pleasure.

THE HYSTERICIZING EGO

The hysteric never perceives his own internal objects or the external objects in the world as they are commonly perceived, but instead transforms their material reality into fantasized reality; in a word, he hystericizes everything. What does it mean to "hystericize"?

We have just seen that, to ensure the state of dissatisfaction, the hysteric seeks in the other the power that oppresses him or the impotence that attracts and disappoints him. Gifted with a keen perceptiveness, he detects in the other the smallest fault, the least sign of weakness, the slightest indication of the other's desire. But his piercing eye is not content to penetrate the appearance of the other to find a point of strength or a chink in the armor, since the hysteric also invents and creates what he perceives. He installs in the other a new body, as libidinally intense and fantasmatic as his own hysterical body. For the body of the hysteric is not his real one, but a body of pure sensation, opening outward like a living animal, a kind of ultra-voracious amoeba that stretches out toward the other, touches him, awakens in him an intense sensation, and feeds on it. To hystericize is to arouse in the other's body a furnace of libido.

Let me now qualify my terminology and be more precise in the definition of the concept of hystericization. What is it to hystericize? To hystericize is to erotize any human expression whatsoever, although in itself it was not sexual by nature. This is exactly what the hysteric does; in all innocence, unknowingly, he sexualizes what is not sexual. He appropriates through the filter of his sexual fantasies—fantasies of which he is not necessarily conscious—every gesture, every word, or every silence that he perceives in the other or that he addresses to the other.

At this point I must add a detail that will hold true each time the word *sexual* is used in this book. What sexuality is in question when we think of hysteria? What is the content of these fantasies? What do we mean when we state that the hysteric sexualizes? Let me first make it clear that the sexual content of hysterical fantasies is never vulgar or pornographic, but rather a very distant and transfigured evocation of sexual behavior. Strictly speaking, these are sensual, not sexual, fantasies, the most innocuous element of which can serve to trigger an autoerotic orgasm.

For we must understand that hysterical sexuality is in no way genital sexuality: it is a sham sexuality, a pseudo-genitality closer to the masturbatory fondling and sexual games of childhood than to an engagement in the direction of actualizing a true sexual relation. To sexualize what is not sexual, as far as the hysteric is concerned, means to transform the most neutral ob-

ject into a sign that evokes and promises a *possible* sexual relation. The hysteric is a remarkable creator of sexual signs that
are rarely followed by the sexual act they announce. His only
pleasure, a masturbatory pleasure, consists in producing these
signs that convince him, and the other, that his true desire is to
enter on the path toward the accomplishment of a sexual act.
And yet, if there is one desire that the hysteric is intent on, it is
that such an act come to naught; more exactly, he is intent on
the unconscious desire for the non-realization of the act and
hence on the desire to remain unsatisfied.

The customary setting of psychoanalysis—the couch, the
ritual of sessions, the particular tone of the analyst's voice, as
well as the transferential bond—constitutes one of the most favorable conditions for the establishment of this active state of
hystericization. The speech of an analysand, male or female,
whether or not he or she bears the diagnosis "hysterical," can at
a given moment in the session take on a sexual meaning, arouse
a fantasy image, and bring about erogenous effects in the body,
be it the body of the analyst or that of the patient himself.

Let us take as an example the words of a female patient who
demonstrates how an innocuous element of reality can be transformed into an erotic sign:

> Every time I hear the click of the main door to the building,
> when you open it for me by pressing your finger on the inter-
> com button, I feel your finger pressing against the skin of
> my arms. And then I laugh at myself. Actually, I laughed only
> the first time that happened. Now I don't laugh any more;
> I'm caught up in what I'm feeling. Whenever I pay attention
> to someone else's slightest movement, I feel it on my skin, I
> feel a warmth on my neck or over my heart. Sometimes I even
> feel aroused when I just hear a man breathing near me. At
> those times something comes straight to my body, with noth-

ing between. Whenever you make the least little sound I feel a sensation of pleasure coming toward my skin. I'm very sensitive to your movements that echo in my skin. I imagine what's going on in you as though I were your own skin all around you. I feel your movements in my skin because I'm your skin. [After a silence, she adds:] It's reassuring to think that, and to tell you about it, and it gives me a boundary. It's the reasoning that's the boundary.

Let us turn now to the third ego state of the hysteric, the sadness ego.

THE SADNESS EGO

We can imagine just how malleable the hysterical ego must be in order to hystericize reality, how it must be able to stretch itself out, with no discontinuity, from the inmost part of its being to the outermost limit of the world, and how uncertain, then, the border becomes that separates internal objects from external ones. But this remarkable plasticity of the ego locates the hysteric in a confused reality, half real and half fantasized, where he becomes involved in the cruel and painful play of multiple, contradictory identifications with various people—and does so at the price of remaining estranged from his own identity, and especially from his identity as a sexed being.

The hysteric can thus identify with a man, with a woman, or even with the fault line between the members of a couple; that is to say he can embody the very discontent that is causing the couple distress. We very frequently note the amazing ease with which the subject assumes the role both of the man and of the woman, and especially the role of the third party who brings about the conflict or resolves it. Whether the hysteric triggers the conflict or calms it, whether he is man or woman, he will invariably take on the role of the excluded one. It is precisely this fact of being cast out into the place of the excluded one that accounts for the sadness that so often overwhelms hysterics. They create a conflictual situation, set dramas in motion, get mixed up in disputes, and once the curtain has fallen they become aware that everything was merely a game from which they have been left out. It is during these characteristic moments of sadness and depression that we find the identification of the hysteric with the suffering peculiar to dissatisfaction: the hysterical subject is no longer a man, no longer a woman; he is now the pain of dissatisfaction. And with this pain he remains unable to say whether he is a man or a woman, to say, simply, what sex he is. The sadness of the hysterical ego corresponds to the emptiness and the uncertainty of his sexual identity.

*
*   *

In short, the way hysteria presents in an analysis (and, beyond analysis, in every relationship with others) is as an unsatisfactory bond—erotizing, sad, entirely polarized around the stubborn refusal to experience pleasure.

It is appropriate to explain at this point that the stubborn refusal to experience pleasure is also to be found at the basis of obsessional and phobic neuroses, but in quite specific forms. What are the obsessional and phobic modalities of the refusal that the neurotic sets up against pleasure? And, by way of comparison, what is the specific modality of the hysterical refusal? That is our next topic of discussion.

DIFFERENTIATING HYSTERIA, OBSESSION, AND PHOBIA

In order to situate hysteria in the larger context of the neuroses, marking out its specificity with regard to the other major clinical categories, we must first of all ask, what is a neurosis in general? The answer is now obvious: neurosis is an inadequate way of defending ourselves, the inappropriate means that we unknowingly employ to confront an unconscious and dangerous pleasure. In so doing we defend ourselves inefficiently because, in order to soothe intolerable pain, we have no recourse other than to transform it into neurotic suffering, into symptoms. When all is said and done we have merely substituted, for a pleasure that is unconscious, dangerous, and implacable, suffering that is conscious, bearable, and, ultimately, reducible. The three classic neuroses can be defined according to the particular manner in which the ego defends itself. There are thus three ways—I emphasize that these are poor ways—of struggling against unbearable pleasure, and hence three different ways of experiencing one's neurosis.

- Suffering neurotically in the *obsessional* manner is suffering consciously in one's thinking, that is, *displacing* unconscious and intolerable pleasure into the suffering of thought.
- *Phobic* suffering is suffering consciously on account of something in the surrounding world, that is, *projecting* outward, onto the external world, the unconscious, unbearable pleasure and crystallizing it in an element of the external environment that has become the threatening phobic object.
- And, finally, suffering in the *hysterical* manner is suffering consciously in the body, that is, *converting* the unconscious and unbearable pleasure into bodily suffering.

> In brief, the unbearable pleasure is converted into somatic distress in hysteria, displaced into disordered thinking in obsessionality, and expelled only to return immediately as an external danger in phobia.

One final comment, based on the illuminating passage in which Freud (1915) notes that what we call hysteria, obsessional neurosis, or paranoia has nothing to do with the unbearable pleasure that is repressed. The terms *hysterical*, *obsessional*, and *phobic* do not, therefore, apply to what is unconscious and repressed, but instead to the types of defense utilized by the ego. Neurosis remains a matter of defense, not a matter of the object against which the defense is set up. Returning to our terminology, we can conclude by stating that there is no neurotic pleasure, obsessional or otherwise; there are only neurotic ways in which the ego defends itself.

2

The Causes of Hysteria

**A READING OF FREUD'S FIRST THEORY:
THE ORIGIN OF HYSTERIA IS THE
PSYCHIC TRACE OF A TRAUMA**

Let us return now to the questions posed at the outset: How does
one become hysterical and what is the cause of hysterical phenomena? By what mechanism is a hysterical symptom formed?
According to Freud's first theory (Freud 1893, 1894, 1896, Freud
and Breuer 1895), hysterical neurosis, and for that matter any
neurosis, comes about through the pathogenic action of a psychic representation, a parasitical idea that is unconscious and
strongly charged with affect. We may recall that at the end of
the nineteenth century, thanks to Charcot and Janet, the thesis
had already been established and relatively well accepted that
hysteria was, as Janet (1894) put it, an illness via representation. Freud, too, took this path but soon went in another direction and introduced a number of modifications, the most decisive
of these being his view that the parasitical idea, the generating

force behind the hysterical symptom, has an essentially sexual content. But what is this sexual idea? How can an unconscious sexual idea, all by itself, possibly bring on aphonia, for example, or bulimia, or even frigidity? By way of response, I shall trace step by step the process that begins with the appearance of this unconscious sexual representation and ends with the appearance of a hysterical symptom in the patient.

At the outset of his career, Freud was convinced—he would later change his mind—that during childhood the hysterical patient had undergone a traumatic experience. The child, taken by surprise, had been the powerless victim of a sexual seduction perpetrated by an adult. The violence of this event lay in the untimely irruption of extreme sexual agitation that flooded the child outside of his conscious awareness. As an immature being, the child remained petrified and mute; he had no time to realize what was happening to him or to experience the anxiety that he would have felt had he been conscious of such brutal turmoil. The violence of the trauma consisted in the emergence of a surplus of sexual affect not experienced in awareness yet registered unconsciously. Thus trauma means an excess of unconscious affect in the absence of the necessary anxiety that, at the time of the incident, would have allowed the child's ego to absorb and tolerate the surplus tension. If trauma occurred, it is because the anxiety that should have arisen was lacking. From that point on, an excess of unassimilable and unbound tension was established in the child's unconscious, tension that did not manage to get discharged in a cry for help, for example, or a motor action of flight. This surplus of affect therefore remained in the ego like a cyst, constituting there the morbid generative source of future hysterical symptoms. The brutal excitation implied by the adult's seductive action introduced into the core of the ego an energy that, transferred from the outside inward, remained enclosed there in the form of an intense, free-floating sexual tension. Such an excess of sexual affect is the equivalent of an unconscious orgasm in an immature being. And so we are to understand that trauma is no longer an external event, but rather a violent internal disturbance within the ego.

There is a further aspect of trauma that requires explanation. A trauma is not only an excess of free-floating tension; it is also an image overactivated by that excess of accumulated sexual energy. The psychic trace of the trauma, which we may now call the *unbearable representation*, thus comprises two unconscious elements: an overload of affect and an overactivated image. We have just seen how the sexual charge arises; now let us look at how the image is created. In order to do so, we must first understand that the ego of the child destined to become a hysteric, the ego that will bear the traumatic impact of the seduction, is a psychic surface made of various bodily images organized like an imaginary body, truly a caricature of the anatomical body. The hysterical ego is thus a body put together in the manner of a harlequin costume, where each diamond shape of the suit corresponds to a distorted image of a particular organ, a limb, an orifice, or some other anatomical part. At the moment of the trauma, the impact of the seduction detaches one of these diamonds, selectively touches one of these images—the one, specifically, that corresponds to the body part jeopardized in the traumatic incident. The surplus of psychic tension is then concentrated on that image, investing it to the point where it becomes dissociated from the rest of the images of the imaginary body, or, what amounts to the same thing, becomes dissociated from the hysterical ego. In characterizing hysteria as an illness via representation, what I have called the unconscious representation or parasitical idea is precisely this unconscious image, disconnected from the imaginary body (the ego), referred to the body part concerned in the traumatic scenario, and highly invested with sexual energy. A detail, a bodily position of the adult seducer,

an odor, a light, a noise: all of these can form the imaginary contents of the representation inscribed in the unconscious, a representation that becomes the focus of the excess of sexual affect.

I want to emphasize once again the essential point of trauma.
It must be kept in mind that the trauma afflicting the child is not
the external aggression but the psychic trace left by the aggression; what counts is not the nature of the impact but its resulting
imprint on the surface of the ego. It is this imprint, this image
highly charged with affect, isolated, painful to the ego, that should
be considered the source of the hysterical symptom, and (even
more generally) the source of any neurotic symptom whatsoever.

The trauma has been displaced. We began by evoking a
traumatic incident external to the child, and now we find the
violence of the invasive attack enclosed within the ego in the
form of an unconscious representation, overcharged with sexual
energy, that is the source of unbearable pain for the ego.

*
* *

HYSTERIA IS BROUGHT ABOUT BY AN
INAPPROPRIATE EGO DEFENSE: REPRESSION

A new question arises at this point: What is the fate of the overload that invests the free-floating representation? How will the
ego get clear of it? And especially: Why is this overcharged representation the morbid origin of hysterical disturbances? The
answer to these questions is fundamental to the understanding
of one of Freud's major theses concerning the etiology of hysteria. According to Freud, hysterical neurosis comes about through

the blundering way in which the ego tries to neutralize that internal parasite that is the unbearable sexual representation. Paradoxically enough, the unbearable representation takes on its full pathogenic force when it is attacked by a struggling ego. It had already been set apart by the weight of its overload, but now the ego isolates it still further, to the point of bringing the tension to a climax. The more the ego attacks the representation, the more it isolates it. This defensive spurt of effort on the part of the ego is precisely what Freud calls *repression*; he placed such strong emphasis on the notion of repression that we often forget that repression primarily means isolation. It is because this representation has been radically separated from the other, organized representations of psychic life that it becomes fundamentally unbearable and maintains an indelible pathogenic activity in the core of the ego. As long as the painful representation is set apart—that is, repressed—the ego will preserve within itself a latent internal psychic trauma.

I want to stress that what makes a hysteric ill is not so much the psychic trace of the trauma, but the fact that this trace, under the force of repression, is overloaded with a surplus of affect that cannot be dissipated. The basic mechanism of hysteria, then, consists in the conflict between, on the one hand, a representation bearing an excess of affect, and, on the other hand, an unfortunate defense, repression, that makes the representation still more virulent. The more repression perseveres against the representation, the more it isolates it and renders it dangerous. In this way the ego becomes exhausted and weak in a vain struggle that leads to the opposite of the intended aim. Repression is such an inadequate defense that we may deem it just as unhealthy for the ego as the pathogenic representation it claims to neutralize.

The role of defense in the etiology of hysteria was so decisive for Freud that he called hysteria *defense hysteria* (we could also call it *repression hysteria*). We shall soon see that Freud would go on to propose a new term: *conversion hysteria*.

*

* *

HYSTERIA IS BROUGHT ABOUT BY THE FAILURE OF REPRESSION: CONVERSION

What we have, then, is a conflict within the ego, between an over-charged representation seeking to discharge its surplus energy and the constant force of repression that, by isolating the representation, prevents it from discharging that surplus. How can this conflict be resolved? As it happens, there will be no radical solution, that is, no liberating discharge, but merely compromise solutions that entail the investment of other representations less dangerous than the unbearable one. What occurs is a displacement of energy, or, more precisely, a transformation of energy from a primary to a secondary state. In order to evade repression, the excess energy passes from its original state—the overinvestment of an unbearable representation—to that other burdensome state that is bodily suffering. The burden is thus transformed, but without ceasing to be an excess of energy with morbid effects.

Now this conflict between overload and repression that we have observed in the attempt to understand the mechanism of hysteria in fact underlies all neuroses. The specificity of each type of neurosis—obsessionality, phobia, and hysteria—depends on the modalities of the final outcome of the conflict. The neurosis will be different according to the type of representation that the overload comes to invest after leaving the intolerable representation. Let me explain what I mean when I say that the outcome of the conflict is decided by the pattern of transformation of the energy into two distinct states. We still have the energic overload in its nature as excess, but this overload assumes two different and successive forms, the first corresponding to the time when it invests the unbearable representation (the traumatic scene), the second to the time when it invests some other representation pertaining to thought (obsessionality), to the external world (phobia), or to the body (hysteria). Even as it preserves its nature as excess, the overload can mobilize itself to bypass repression in three possible ways, in other words, to bring about three failures of repression. These, in the end, are three poor solutions, since each of them gives rise to a neurotic symptom that causes suffering.

Obsessionality

In the first possible outcome, the burden is displaced, leaving the painful representation in order to establish itself in thought and overinvesting a conscious idea that intrudes in the life of the neurotic. We recognize here the formative mechanism of the obsessional's perseverative idea.

Phobia

The second outcome is that of phobic neurosis. Here, too, the burden leaves the representation, but instead of establishing itself immediately in an element of thought, as is the case in obsessionality, it at first remains at large, unattached, waiting in the ego. The charge, floating and available, is then projected onto the external world, becoming fixed on a definite element (crowds, an animal, enclosed space, tunnels, etc.) that thenceforth becomes the object that the phobic person must flee in order to avoid the emergence of anxiety.

SUFFERING IN THE CONVERSION SYMPTOM IS THE EQUIVALENT OF MASTURBATORY GRATIFICATION

Conversion

The third outcome that foils repression, the one we are concerned with here, consists in the transformation of the excessive sexual charge into a nervous impulse, likewise excessive, that, acting as a stimulant or an inhibitor, gives rise to somatic distress. Thus conversion is defined, from an economic point of view, as the transformation of a constant energic excess as it passes from a psychic to a somatic state. This leap from the psyche to the soma, which remains an open question nowadays (Benoit 1985), can be described as follows. The energic overload breaks free of the unbearable representation, retains its nature as excess, and re-emerges transformed into bodily suffering, whether in the form of painful hypersensitivity or in the form of a sensory or motor inhibition. Since the excess of energy passing from the psyche to the soma remains constant—that is, always inordinate—we may suppose that the suffering of a bodily symptom is energically equivalent to the excitation of the original trauma, or, more precisely, equivalent to that excess of sexual affect that we have compared to orgasm.

This orgasm is, strictly speaking, the kind achieved through masturbation, since we must not forget that the hysteric's sexuality remains essentially infantile. A sudden blush appearing on the neck of a given hysterical patient at the end of a session may be considered, from the psychoanalytic point of view, to be the cutaneous equivalent of an orgasm. Atypical vomiting, enuresis in a child, a crying fit, muteness, or a hysterical paralysis of the gait—when all is said and done, these constitute the roundabout and neurotic way in which the hysteric experiences his infantile sexuality. Conversion symptoms are thus to be taken as the physical equivalents of infantile masturbatory satisfactions.

Of the three failures of repression, then—the failure through displacement of the overload of a representation onto an idea in obsessional neurosis, the failure through projection of the overload from the interior of the psyche onto the external world in phobia, and the failure through conversion of the overload into a somatic symptom—the last is the distinctive mechanism of hysteria. Thus for the term *defense hysteria* Freud came to prefer the expression *conversion hysteria*.

*

* *

THE CHOICE OF ORGAN TO BE THE SITE OF CONVERSION

It is clear that in order to foil repression and evade its force, the surplus energy has to find a solution consisting in bodily conversion and investment of a particular organ. But how does the choice of this organ come about? How does it happen that the overload irrupts into one bodily area rather than another? The somatic region affected by the conversion symptom corresponds precisely to that part of the body that was previously stricken by the trauma and has thus become a specific image. In conversion, the energic charge abandons the unconscious image and energizes the organ of which this image is the reflection. The choice of the somatic conversion site can therefore be explained very schematically according to the following sequence: *from the part of the body perceived in the traumatic episode (for example, the arm), to the unconscious image of an arm, to conversion paralysis of the arm.*

Of course, these three successive bodily states—perceived body, imagined body, and suffering body—do not always refer only to the body of one and the same person. The bodily region perceived during the traumatization may equally well belong to the child's body, to that of the adult seducer, or even to the body of a witness to the scene. The important point is not whose body it is, but what body part was most vividly and meaningfully perceived by the child at the time of the trauma. If, for example, during the traumatic seduction scene the outraged shouting of a witness was heard—as in the case of a horrified mother happening on the stepfather fondling her daughter's body—the conversion symptom will take the form of an inhibition of the voice (aphonia) that will afflict the girl when, later, she has become a hysterical woman. The mother's shouting, perceived and inscribed in the child's unconscious, will re-emerge later on as a loss of voice. The hysteric actualizes in her body (as aphonia) the psychic imprint of the other's body (the mother's shouting).

*

* *

If we sum up the two essential aspects of conversion—the constancy of the energic excess passing from the psychosexual state to that of somatic suffering, and the persistence of an area of the body passing from the state of unconscious image to that of organic conversion—we can understand why conversion is a poor and inappropriate solution. The energy, to be sure, has changed systems, but the subject continues to suffer because the reason for his suffering remains unchanged. On the psychic level or the somatic, he suffers from having within him an unassimilable and irreducible excess. Conversion is an inefficient solution because it does not resolve the main difficulty underlying hysteria, namely the confinement of a surplus of energy within an element isolated and detached from the whole, whether this be a psychic representation or a somatic conversion. The outcome of conversion is unfortunate because the problem of incompatibility remains unaltered: at first there was the incompatibility of the representation with the remainder of the representations constituting the ego of the hysteric, and now this has turned into the incompatibility of somatic suffering that does not obey the laws of the real body.

But a question soon arises. Since conversion is not a good solution, could there be some other, better way of dealing with the excess? A solution other than a change of state in the course of which, as we have seen, the excess still persists? Yes: it would be to divide up and distribute this excess into a multiplicity of representations, to collectivize the excess—in short, to defuse it by dispersing it. But how? At this point we can begin to consider the listening of the analyst as just such a dispersal of the excess, a possible way to cure the subject of what has been irreconcilable within him.

*
*   *

THE CONVERSION SYMPTOM DISAPPEARS IF IT TAKES ON A SYMBOLIC VALUE PRODUCED BY THE ANALYST'S LISTENING

> *It is because someone is listening to me and wants to discover the enigma of the discomfort in my body that this discomfort will come to make sense in my history; then maybe one day it will disappear.*

Since, as we have seen, conversion is not a good solution, how, then, to handle the excess and cure the hysteric of the irreconciliation that eats away at him? I propose the following hypothesis: the analyst's listening and interpretation serve as a symbolic ego, that is, as a cohesive set of representations. The point is that this is an ego capable of accommodating the irreconcilable representation that the hysterical ego represses, thereby neutralizing the morbid overload by distributing it among the set of its own representations. The analyst's listening integrates and disperses what the hysteric represses and concentrates. In this way the subject is cured of the irreconcilable, and the conversion symptom will be able to vanish.

I am setting forth here, in exact terms and in the vocabulary of energic theory, the general principle that a conversion symptom diminishes if it takes on the symbolic value conferred on it by the analyst's listening and interpretation. When a symptom assumes a symbolic value and becomes able to disappear, the irreconcilable representation for which the symptom was a substitute has become integrated into the system of representations of the analytic listening, its surplus having been discharged. I am making the same observation expressed in two different modes, the one energic, the other symbolic. To say that the irreconcilable representation is integrated within the listening ego is the same as saying that the analyst's listening gives a symbolic meaning to the conversion symptom and causes it to disappear. Analytic listening thus operates in both the energic and the symbolic registers.

Now, it is clear that a conversion symptom will assume a symbolic meaning and will disappear only on condition that it is uttered by the patient and received by listening—not by listening that reveals a hidden meaning already present, but one that generates a new meaning. But how can it be that an analyst's silent and apparently passive listening can, all by itself, produce meaning, and that the production of this meaning will cause the symptom to vanish? Listening can indeed have the power of generating a new meaning if it is the listening of an analyst whose desire is concave, receptive to the impact of a symptomatic utterance. Let me be clear: it is not enough for the patient to name his conversion symptom and speak about it to others in order for it to take on meaning. The listening that receives this speech must also be transferential, that is, the listening of a therapist who desires to enter into the patient's psyche to the point of embodying the irreducible excess inside it, making himself the nucleus of the suffering. If he is successful, if his desire as analyst is in that place, identified with the cause of the suffering, then he will be led to make the interpretation or to cause it to arise indirectly in the patient's words. What is most important is that the analyst identify with the unassimilable excess, become the energy itself, if he is to find himself drawn toward making the interpretation. There is no need to search in books or to cogitate in order to make the right interpretation; it will arise spontaneously if the practitioner has first managed to lodge himself in the psychic core of the excess. Identify with the nucleus of the suffering and the interpretation will spring forth—and when it arrives, it will offer itself as a substitute for the unbearable representation, a substitute radically different from the one provided by the conversion symptom.

Before the listening, the irreconcilable representation was spoken by the symptom via the conversion, and that caused suffering; with the listening, the same representation is spoken by the interpretation, and this dispels suffering. Why? Because the analyst, uttering the irreconcilable representation through the interpretation, enables the excess borne by the representation to disperse into the group of representations embodied by the analytic listening (the symbolic ego). Onto the hysteric's exhausted ego, ill from the futile attempt at repression, I as psychoanalyst graft my desire to be the suffering of the symptom, and by means of the interpretation I reconcile the representation that up to now has been unassimilable. In this way, the symptom becomes compatible with the rest of the body and is able to disappear. With my listening, that is, with my unconscious, I take upon myself the integration of what the hysterical ego rejects. This desire on the part of the analyst, though it is silent and unspoken, is enough to enable his listening to confer symbolic value on the symptom and thereby cause it to vanish. Yes, listening confers meaning, and meaning kills the symptom because it renders it ordinary and banal, assigning it a place in the constellation of events comprising the subject's psychic life. As long as it was unheard, the symptom remained a thorn in the flesh, unassimilable; listening was needed in order to give it signification, so that the suffering could diminish and the symptom gradually dissolve.

In short, it is as though the analyst's listening functions as a family of representations welcoming the irreconcilable representation that up to now was repressed by the hysterical ego. The surplus energy is thereby spread out among the different members of this auxiliary family that is the symbolic ego in its role as listening. Freed of the overload and assimilated to its sister representations, the formerly irreconcilable representation, now calmed, will finally be able to reintegrate the ego that had cast it out. Analytic listening thus acts as an intermediary, a detour by means of which the irreconcilable representation becomes reconciled—an intermediary between a sick ego that represses and a new ego, no longer hysterical, that from now on accepts. In structural terms, the set of representations that represses (called the *hysterical ego*), the set of representations that welcomes (called the *symbolic ego*, that is, psychoanalytic listening), and the set of representations of a *new ego* that now accepts constitute three overlapping sets within the framework of the transference. They are all based on one and the same structure called the unconscious, an unconscious that belongs to neither of the analytic partners.

*
* *

A READING OF FREUD'S SECOND THEORY: THE ORIGIN OF HYSTERIA IS AN UNCONSCIOUS FANTASY

> *The interest of the student of hysteria soon turns from the symptoms to the fantasies that give rise to them.*
>
> Freud

Before continuing, let me start with a question: Is this theory that I have been developing from my reading of Freud's initial formulations still valid today? Can we still make use of it in our work with our patients? When a psychoanalyst nowadays encounters a hysterical conversion symptom—a somatic problem such as often comes up in analysis, an outbreak of hives, for example, or dizzy spells in a child—does he think in the terms we have been using? I would not hesitate to say yes. The theory of conversion, as I have interpreted it, remains extremely current today, all the more so if we conceptualize it according to the modification Freud introduced in 1905a: the origin of hysteria is no longer a representation but an unconscious fantasy. And what is converted is fantasized anxiety and no longer an overload of the representation.

For, according to Freud's view at this later time, it is not necessary to find a real traumatic event in the patient's history in order to explain the appearance of a conversion symptom. The painful representation no longer needs to stem from a past sexual seduction by an adult. It is enough, now, to think of our childhood, to imagine the development of our bodily drives, and to understand that each experience undergone in childhood on the level of the different erogenous zones—mouth, anus, muscles, skin, eyes—has the precise value of a *trauma*. Without having to go through a real traumatic experience prompted by an external agent, the infantile ego, during its entire sexual maturation, is itself the natural site of the violent and spontaneous appearance of an excessive tension called desire.

But where can we locate, in the normal evolution of our libidinal body, this spontaneous appearance of a trauma produced without external intervention? For Freud, and for us today, the term *trauma* no longer refers essentially to an external event; it designates a psychic event charged with affect, a true local micro-trauma centering around an erogenous area of the body and consisting in the fabrication of a traumatic scene that psychoanalysis calls a *fantasy*. Needless to say, the fact that the fantasy is a trauma does not mean that all traumas are fantasies. In the daily life of the child there can occur real traumatic shocks caused by external agents; these exist and frequently lead to consultations in child analysis. In such cases, the affect arising from the real trauma is terror that, though not repressed, nonetheless remains inscribed in one form or another in the fantasy life of the infantile psyche. So let me be clear: of course there are traumas that are not fantasies, but every trauma, be it real or psychic, is necessarily inscribed in fantasy life.

But we must go further. Why say that fantasies are equivalent to traumas? Because in this hotbed of fantasy that is the erogenous zone there springs forth an excess of sexuality, nongenital (that is, autoerotic) and automatically subject to the force of repression. Infantile sexuality always gets off to a bad start because it is inordinate and extreme. This is the great discovery that led Freud to abandon the theory of actual trauma as the origin of hysteria. Infantile sexuality is an unconscious center of suffering, since it is always excessive in relation to the limited physical and psychic means of the child. A child inevitably remains premature, unprepared, with regard to the tension that arises in its body, and this libidinal tension is too intense for its ego. As the source of future symptoms, infantile sexuality is traumatic and pathogenic because of its overactivity.

According to the first theory, the actual traumatic incident underlying hysteria involved the perverse action of an adult on a passive child. Now the perspective is reversed: it is the child's own erogenous body that gives rise to the psychic event, since this body is a center of teeming sexuality, the site of desire. The desire contains within it the idea that one day it will achieve the fulfillment of an unlimited, absolute pleasure. What the subject finds intolerable is just this possibility of an absolute fulfillment of desire. As I said at the outset, pleasure is intolerable for the subject because, if he were to experience it, it would jeopardize the integrity of his entire being. The upsurge of the excess of sexuality, called desire, with the possibility of its fulfillment, called pleasure, is so intense that it must be moderated by the unconscious creation of fictions, of protective scenarios and fantasies.

These fantasmatic formulations, produced outside of the subject's awareness, are thus the psychic response necessary for containing the excess energy that is the thrust of desire. A fantasy scene, as "true" as the former traumatic scene occurring in reality, will henceforth give dramatic shape to the desirous tension. When this tension is fantasized, that is, tempered by fantasy, it remains just as unendurable, but it is integrated and circumscribed in the fantasy scenario. It is what we call fantasmatic anxiety. Anxiety is the name for desire and pleasure when they are inscribed in the framework of fantasy.

Now, whether the excess energy is a surplus of affect resulting from a traumatic shock (the first theory), or a fantasmatic anxiety corresponding to the spontaneous and premature awakening of infantile sexuality (the new theory of fantasy), what remains constant is the thesis that the primary cause of hysteria is to be found in the unconscious activity of an overinvested representation—with the exception, in the latter case, that the contents of this representation are no longer reduced to the limited image of a body part, as in the first theory, but instead are deployed according to a dramatic scenario called a fantasy. This fantasy is played out in a short theatrical sequence that always comprises the following elements: a main action, the protagonists, and a bodily region (the source of anxiety) that is overinvested. In the new theory, the fantasy constructed in this way is just as unconscious and subject to repression as was the unbearable representation of the first theory, and, like that representation, the fantasy carries with it an intolerable excess of affect, an excess that we may now call anxiety. This anxiety, evading repression, will find its ultimate expression in somatic distress. Now that Freud's second theory has placed fantasy at the origin of hysteria, analysts no longer need to search for a datable, real traumatic event underlying the symptom; what we look for instead is the "trauma" of an anxious fantasy.

3

The Sexual Life of the Hysteric

**THE SEXUAL LIFE OF THE HYSTERIC IS
A PARADOX, THE PAINFUL EXPRESSION OF
AN UNCONSCIOUS FANTASY**

> *Desire and disgust are the two columns of the temple of Living.*
> Valéry

But what is this unconscious fantasy at the source of hysteria? Who are its actors, how do they act, and what is the anxiety that animates them? Before answering, I want to begin by considering the clinical effects that this fantasy produces in the sexual life of hysterical patients. For the disorders of hysterical sexuality may be understood as the most direct manifestation, or, to be more precise, the most immediate somatic conversion, of the anxiety governing the originary fantasy of hysteria. We shall see later on what this fantasy is and what anxiety it involves. For the moment, let us observe that there are two different types of conversion that, far from being mutually exclusive, complement one another: a global conversion transforming anxiety into a general bodily state, and a local conversion transforming anxiety into a somatic problem limited to a particular body part. In my view, the idea of a global conversion, affecting the body as a whole and not limited to a given part, offers a more adequate account of hysterical sexuality. I believe that when we begin to think in terms of *unconscious fantasy* instead of representation (image of a body part), in terms of *anxiety* instead of excess of energy, Freud's revised theory of conversion is even more fruitful as an explanation of the sexual suffering of hysteria. It allows us to assert that the anxiety of the fantasy is transformed into a state of distress in the hysteric's sexual life, a state of suffering due to a general erotization of the body, paradoxically accompanied by inhibition and anesthesia in the genital zone.

*
*   *

THE PARADOX OF THE HYSTERIC'S SEXUAL LIFE

I want to specify that this genital inhibition is expressed in the hysteric's sexual life not, as one might think, by indifference to sexuality, but most often by an aversion, a real disgust, toward all carnal contact. It is not a retreat, but an active movement of repulsion—a repulsion so characteristic that Freud did not hesitate to say that he considered hysterical anyone who reacted with disgust to a sexual stimulus, even if no somatic symptoms were present (Freud and Breuer 1895). A global hypererotization of the non-genital body paradoxically coexists alongside a deep aversion to genital coitus. Impotence, premature ejaculation, vaginismus, and frigidity are all disorders characteristic of the sexual life of the hysteric, who, in one way or another, experiences the man's unconscious anxiety about penetrating a woman's body and the woman's unconscious anxiety about letting herself be penetrated. The paradox of the hysteric when it comes to sexuality is that these are men and women who, on the one hand, are overpreoccupied with sex, who attempt to erotize all their social relationships, but who, on the other hand, suffer—without knowing why—when they have to undergo the ordeal of a genital encounter with the opposite sex. I am thinking, for example, of the sort of men who are concerned about the size and the qualities of their penises, or about their muscular attractiveness, but who, at the same time, show little interest in women, or, more precisely, little urge to penetrate a woman's body. These are narcissistic, exhibitionistic men, sometimes quite seductive, with varying degrees of homosexuality and masturbatory activity.

*
*   *

THE HYSTERICAL WOMAN AND THE PLEASURE IN OPENNESS

When we turn to hysterical women, this paradox seems much more complicated and obscure. For, as it happens, the large number of amorous adventures that certain women have contrasts with their suffering, a suffering evident in different kinds of inhibitions (frigidity, vaginismus, etc.), during the sexual act. Among these inhibitions there is an essential and secret one that affects the hysteric at the center of her being as a woman. Even as she conducts an apparently happy sexual relationship with a man, the hysterical woman can refuse—almost unbeknownst to herself but yet with determination—to open herself to the sexual presence of the other's body. The lesson drawn by psychoanalysis from this refusal of the hysterical woman is that she offers herself but does not give herself over to the experience; she is able to have sexual relations with vaginal or clitoral orgasm while remaining disengaged with regard to her essence as a woman. At the moment when she is confronted with the threat of losing this fundamental virginity, she withdraws from the threshold of orgasmic pleasure, holding herself back from experiencing a radically different pleasure, enigmatic and dangerous, that we may call the pleasure in openness.* The hysteric can offer herself to orgasm, but nonetheless does not abandon herself to the pleasure in openness.

Very well then, she does not give herself over, but a question remains: Is it possible, hysterical or not, truly to abandon oneself to this infinite pleasure? Is it conceivable to take pleasure in openness? Apart from mystics and their ecstatic experiences, perhaps we are all, like hysterics, beings for whom the sexual relation remains ultimately impossible. Certainly this is what Lacan tried to demonstrate in all his writings. But then what would characterize the hysteric in particular, if not the intensity and the passion with which she clashes with and injures herself against the limit of an impossible sexual relation?

In refusing to surrender, hysterics inevitably find themselves drawn toward discontent. Whether it is the man who demonstrably refuses to penetrate a woman, or the woman who, while accepting penetration, refuses to give up her essential virginity,

---

*The concept of openness has been extensively developed by Audouard (1984).

both live in a permanent and latent state of dissatisfaction. This dissatisfaction is not confined to sexual matters but extends to the totality of life, and does so, sometimes in a very painful way, through depressive episodes or even suicide attempts. And yet despite this pain, surprisingly enough, the hysteric clings to his discontent. He values it to the point of making it his desire: the desire for dissatisfaction, the desire that Lacan has forever marked out as the distinctive feature of hysteria. The hysteric desires to be dissatisfied because dissatisfaction guarantees the fundamental inviolability of his being. The more discontented he is, the better he is protected from the threat of a pleasure perceived as entailing a risk of disintegration and madness.

4

Hysterical Fantasies

THE UNCONSCIOUS FANTASY AT THE ROOT OF HYSTERIA IS A VISUAL FANTASY—THE THREAT OF CASTRATION ENTERS THROUGH THE EYES: THE CASE OF A BOY

But what is the reason for this paradox of the hysteric's sexual life, for excessive and painful erotization of the non-genital body and inhibition of the genital zone along with the resulting dissatisfaction? I have already mentioned that the origin of this splitting in hysterical sexuality is an unconscious fantasy. The question was: Who are the actors in this originary fantasy of hysteria, how do they act, and—above all—what is the nature of the anxiety that passes through them? To give the answer straightaway, the fantasy underlying hysterical neurosis, the fantasy that, regardless of the various forms in which it may appear, any analyst will be able to observe in working with a hysterical patient, can be summed up briefly in the following scenario:

A boy (the case of a girl will be presented further on) is filled with dread *at the sight of* the nude body of a woman, specifically the "castrated" body of the mother or of any other woman with whom he has a loving relationship. The vision of the female body, perceived as a body deprived of a penis, causes anxiety because the child thinks that he may be the victim of a similar castration. All that is needed for the boy to fear this fate is to see his mother naked and perceive her as castrated.

Let us recall that the prohibition against incest uttered by the voice of the father is the complement of this other prohibition, silent and visual, imposed by the nakedness of the maternal body. These two threats, the one from the mother's body entering through the eyes, the other from the father's voice entering through the ears, undoubtedly converge to produce castration anxiety.

*

* *

FANTASIED ANXIETY DESTINED TO BE EXPRESSED IN A CONVERSION SYMPTOM IS THE UNBEARABLE ANXIETY CALLED "CASTRATION ANXIETY"

The psychic life of the hysteric is therefore organized around this visual fantasy that unfolds in a linear path starting from the boy's eyes, then touching the sexual hole of the castrated Other, and finally returning toward the boy's own phallus. The child's gaze is pleasure and horror at the same time, the pleasure of visual curiosity as he uncovers his mother's lack, and horror as he infers that, if the lack has befallen the mother, he himself can be castrated. This horror, the dominant affect of the boy's hysterical fantasy, is what psychoanalysis calls *castration anxiety*. Such anxiety should, strictly speaking, be called anxiety in the face of the *threat* of castration, since it refers not to the pain of undergoing castration but to the fear of perceiving the threat of it. Castration anxiety means fear of the threat of visually perceived castration, not fear of being castrated in reality. The only figure who is truly castrated in the fantasy scenario of hysteria is the mother; castration always pertains to the other.

CASTRATION ANXIETY IS UNCONSCIOUS

One further observation on the unconscious nature of castration anxiety: when the analyst uses this expression, we must not confuse it with the anxiety that we observe, for example, in children with various fears such as nightmares, night terrors, and so forth. Such disturbances, marked by anxiety in actual life and experienced by the child in the form of fear, are only the clinical manifestations of an invisible struggle carried on by the ego against the unconscious castration anxiety inherent in the fantasy. Consciously experienced anxiety, called fear, is thus the outward sign of repression, the ego defense against that other fantasmatic anxiety, not consciously experienced, that we call castration anxiety. Of course—and this is the Freudian thesis that I have been maintaining throughout—unconscious castration anxiety is the source not only of these fears but of all neurotic phenomena.

Let me be more precise with regard to terminology. At this time it may be useful to bring together the various expressions

I have used to designate the unconscious, repressed, unbearable matter that the hysterical ego is called upon to convert. I have just been speaking of *unconscious castration anxiety*. But at the outset, in the context of the theory of trauma, I designated the unconscious matter as *overload of the unconscious representation*. What must be kept in mind is that the unconscious matter that is converted is, from the point of view of trauma theory, the energic overload, and, from the point of view of fantasy theory, castration anxiety. One further point needs to be made in order to clarify the difference between the unbearable anxiety of castration and unbearable pleasure. The former is anxiety about the threat of a castration bearing on a limited *part* of the body, the phallus. The latter is the fear and refusal of a limitless pleasure threatening the integrity of the *entire* being. Either I am anxious about the idea of risking my phallus, or I am afraid of losing my being if I fulfill my incestuous desire.

THE HYSTERICAL FANTASY IS AN "ARREST AT THE IMAGE" IN THE PHALLIC STAGE OF THE CHILD'S LIBIDINAL DEVELOPMENT

According to Freud, the visual fantasy-scenario of hysteria I have just been describing corresponds in all respects to a fictive scene supposedly witnessed by a 5-year-old child in the phallic stage of his libidinal development. *The hysteric, then, is the child who has not progressed beyond this stage but remains fixated there.* This is the phallic stage because the sexual part that the mother lacks in the image of her body is not, in the child's eyes, the penis, but the idol of the penis, the fiction of a powerful penis charged with the utmost libidinal tension, a simulacrum of the penis that psychoanalysis conceptualizes with the term *phallus*. To be precise, when the boy makes the anxious discovery that his mother is deprived of the phallus, his universe—hitherto inhabited only by beings who, like him, possess the phallus—is split into two classes of beings, those who are bearers of a phallus and those who have been divested of it, and this has nothing to do with their anatomical sex. At the phallic stage, the child has not yet learned the difference between the male sex and the female sex; the infantile universe is divided into beings who either have the phallus or are deprived of it, or, simply, into powerful and powerless beings, the healthy and the sick, the beautiful and the ugly, not into men who have penises and women who have vaginas. In other words, the child submerged in this universe does not know whether it is a boy or a girl. Precisely this sexual uncertainty underlies the suffering of the hysteric.

We may note here that libidinal intensity in the penile and clitoral areas and the need for reassurance about the permanence and the integrity of one's sexual organ explain the tendency in the phallic-stage child, and later in the hysteric, toward frequent and compulsive masturbation.

*
*   *

THE VISUAL FANTASY OF CASTRATION AS THE UNCONSCIOUS ORIGIN OF HYSTERIA: THE CASE OF A GIRL

At this point I can hear a woman reader asking me: "All right; I understand that the boy is made anxious by the danger posed by the image of a castrated mother, but what about the girl, the girl I once was?" By way of an answer I shall set forth my own ideas about the female castration fantasy. But first let us recall the classic Freudian position. According to Freud, the affect that informs the female castration fantasy at the root of hysteria is not anxiety, as in the case of the boy, but hatred and resentment toward the mother. A woman cannot experience castration anxiety in the true sense of the term; since she is already castrated, she need not fear it. All the same, there is a female castration fantasy, one in which castration is not a threat but an accomplished fact. In her fantasy, the girl has the concept not of the penis, but of a phallus that has been stolen from her. And she thinks, not of the vagina as a positive cavity, but of the lack of a phallus that should have been there.

Let us outline, as in the case of the boy, the moment of the fantasmatic scene, but this time in the feminine version:

The girl, too, makes the visual discovery of her mother's nude body and says to herself: "Oh! I'm castrated just like her!" Let us not forget that before this discovery, the girl, having seen a boy's penis, had been under the impression that all human beings possessed this powerful thing called the phallus. Taken aback by the castrated body of her mother and forced to acknowledge her own castration, the girl is seized by a strong wish to have this phallus that she lacks, or to see her own little clitoral phallus get bigger one day. Caught up in this envy, she suddenly feels a rush of vengeful hatred toward her mother, whom she holds responsible for having made her a girl and for having been unable to protect her by guaranteeing her the permanence of phallic power.[1]

---

1. For a fuller version of the female castration fantasy, see Nasio 1988, pp. 23–51.

This scenario follows the general outline of the classic Freudian view of the female castration fantasy. But we really ought to characterize this fantasy more precisely and call it the female fantasy of ascertaining an *already accomplished castration*. For the boy, on the other hand, what we saw was the male fantasy of a threat of *feared castration in the future*. To complete the picture, we must add that the girl's hostility toward her castrated mother revives an older feeling of hatred, the bitterness that accompanied the painful separation of weaning.

However, on the basis of our clinical experience with hysterical patients, we can introduce a modification in the Freudian thesis. For in fact the clinical confirmation of the paradox of hysterical sexuality, and in particular of that strange variant of sexual inhibition involving renunciation of the pleasure of penetration, has led us to a new conceptualization of the female castration fantasy underlying hysteria. Here we encounter some of Ernest Jones's (1913) ideas. Before the moment when she discovers the castrated mother, the girl, who attributes a universal phallus to all human beings, is already aware of obscure sensations in her lower abdomen and her vagina with the same mixture of physical sensations, narcissism, and daydreaming that the penis arouses in the boy. While for Freud the phallus, in the case of the girl, could be localized in her clitoris at a certain stage of her development, we may extend this localization to the other female genital organs and in particular to the uterus. According to this view, the little girl invests her clitoris and her internal sexual organs in the same way the boy invests his penile organ, that is, with the same phallic power and the same fear of feeling them threatened.[2]

---

2. Admittedly, these are *internal* organs that the girl invests in the same manner as the boy invests his *external* penile organ. But there remains the

Thus, just as the boy considers his penis to be a phallus that must never be lost, the girl regards her genital organs as a phallus to preserve from any attack. What happens is that the sight of the mother's naked and imposing body awakens in the little girl concern about a danger threatening the integrity of her genital organs, especially her uterus. The maternal body presents itself to the girl-child's eyes as immense, monstrous, splendid, one big anxiety-provoking phallus. I do not deny that the girl experiences resentment and disappointment with regard to her mother, but I also want to recognize and validate the *anxiety* aroused by this inordinate and intrusive phallus that is the body of the mother-phallus. "Mother-phallus," not "phallic mother," since what we are dealing with is not a mother who has a phallus, but a mother entirely assimilated to, identified with, a phallus that cannot be surpassed.[3]

This, then, is my proposal. It is my belief that the early anxiety aroused by the danger of a mother-phallus is the unconscious source of the anxiety that a hysterical woman can experience during sexual penetration, anxiety that she apprehends as the risk of tearing and bursting her uterus, her vagina, and, ultimately, her entire being. In her fantasy, the man's penis is the unconscious equivalent of the inordinate and dangerous maternal body.

---

interesting question of telling the difference between the one and the other with regard to the manner of perceiving and investing one's own organs. It is as if the girl has a more acute perception of internal sensations (proprioceptive perception) than the boy, and perhaps, inversely, as if the boy is more sensitive than the girl when it comes to perception of external forms.

3. I also want to mention here, without going into detail, the existence of another category of feminine anxiety, one that, according to Freud, becomes the focus of all of a woman's anxieties, namely the loss of the love object.

*
*   *

WHAT IS HYSTERICAL CONVERSION?
A PHALLICIZATION OF THE NON-GENITAL BODY
AND ESTRANGEMENT FROM THE GENITAL BODY

In their intense anxiety over the threat to what they consider the essential part of themselves, their phallus, hysterics of either sex lose their way in the confusion of not knowing whether they are men or women. In a word, the phallic universe constitutes the anxiety-ridden world in which hysterical subjects endlessly struggle. The more they are uncertain of their sexual identity, the more they cling to the phallus, and the greater their anxiety becomes until finally it is transformed into symptoms and suffering.

I raised the question earlier of how to explain the paradox of the hysteric's sexual life as well as the dissatisfaction that results from it. Now an answer can be given. This permanent haunting by fantasmatic dangers that threaten the integrity of his entire being is a source of unbearable anxiety—unconsciously unbearable—that he has to get rid of. Now, the hysteric is hysterical precisely because of the means he uses to get rid of his anxiety. How does he do it? We are already familiar with an initial response formulated in terms of trauma theory, since we have looked at conversion as a failure of repression, a failure brought about by the displacement of the overload of the irreconcilable representation onto other representations. Because the ego, as we have seen, is unable to free itself of the overload by means of a liberating discharge, it displaces it, that is, converts it, by investing a body part.

But the theory of the fantasmatic origin of hysteria that we have started to examine, along with the concept of the phallus and the concept of castration anxiety, has led us to think of the mechanism of conversion in an entirely different way. And here we have an additional reason to theorize conversion differently, and that is the need to explain not only the local formation of a symptom, but also the generalized bodily suffering of the hysteric and, still more specifically, the paradox of his sexual life and its attendant discontent. It is clear that, far from being mutually exclusive, these two possible ways of understanding the mechanism of local and global conversion complement each other closely in offering an account of the clinical picture of hysteria.

Let us pause, therefore, to look at the second way of explaining the mechanism of conversion. We know that the conversion of castration anxiety gives rise to a twofold clinical effect, an excitation affecting the whole of the body globally, and an inhibition affecting the genital region in a circumscribed fashion. But what is the impulse behind this transformation? Let us go back for a moment to the internal dynamics of the unconscious castration fantasy. What we find there is that the entire body, by which I mean all the libidinal tension of the fantasied body, becomes concentrated in one sole place that, in the vocabulary of medical anatomy, would be called the genital area, but that, in fantasy, is called the phallus.

To be sure, we must not forget that the eyes, which are also a heavily invested erogenous zone, also accumulate tension. For it is with his eyes that the child of the fantasy experiences the pleasure and the horror of perceiving the mother's castration. But the eyes are merely a tributary, channeling the libido toward that central nucleus that is the phallus. All energy is there, in the phallus, collected in that teeming core of confused sensations, harrowing excitations, and inordinate affects, the core from which all forces radiate out and in which are hidden all the weaknesses called anxiety. But how, then, can this excess of unassimilable energy, all this phallic libido, this mixture of love and anxiety subject to the insistent force of repression—how can it find an outlet? How can the ego dispose of it, if not by diverting it away from the phallic nucleus as one diverts the course of a river?

The phenomenon of conversion can, in effect, be compared to movement between connected vessels. Phallic libido contained in one vessel—the unconscious castration fantasy—flows into another vessel that represents the real suffering body of the hysteric. The libido, formerly accumulated in the fantasied phallus, leaves this central source and gradually phallicizes the real body; that is, it spreads throughout this body, with the isolated exception of the so-called genital zone. Whereas, in the unconscious, the body had condensed and reduced itself to the point of being only the phallus, now, in reality, the entire body of the hysteric is invaded by the phenomenon of phallicization. The real body thus becomes a body suffering from being one huge phallus. The mechanism of conversion can now be understood: what takes place is a phallicization of the non-genital body and, simultaneously, an estrangement from the genital body. The hysteric's body, therefore, suffers from being an outsized, cumbersome phallus with a hole in it in the genital region, as in Figure 4–1.

WHAT IS CONVERTED IN HYSTERICAL CONVERSION? CASTRATION ANXIETY IS CONVERTED PARTLY INTO EXCESSIVE EROTIZATION OF THE NON-GENITAL BODY, PARTLY (AND PARADOXICALLY) INTO INHIBITION OF GENITAL SEXUALITY

At this point it is easier to understand why, in their hysterical position, both sexes have the most compelling reasons to deny any idea of a sexual relation, to anesthetize their genital organs,

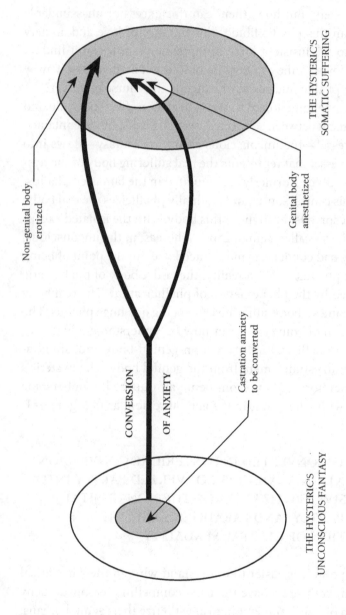

Non-genital body erotized

THE HYSTERIC'S SOMATIC SUFFERING

Genital body anesthetized

CONVERSION

OF ANXIETY

Castration anxiety to be converted

THE HYSTERIC'S UNCONSCIOUS FANTASY

Figure 4–1. The Hysterical Conversion of Castration Anxiety into Somatic Suffering

and, in contrast, to phallicize their bodies globally. The genital zone becomes an emptied-out, disused place, while the non-genital body becomes aroused and erect like a powerful phallus, a place of narcissistic veneration, object of all seductions, but also the site of much suffering. The non-genital body is converted into this phallus that the hysteric has become: he is phallus. We can see that to have the phallus, for a hysteric, is in reality to be it. But what phallus is he? The one that was missing in the mother, in the castrated other of the castration fantasy.

Now we can understand the source of the suffering that the hysteric experiences. The subject suffers from having been transformed into that phallus of which the other has been castrated. He is that which the other does not have, and that is painful. For this superfluity of narcissism, this phallicism spread throughout the body, constitutes such an excess that even if it gives the subject the feeling that he exists, it does so at the painful cost of leaving him forever prey to the most innocuous stimuli from the external world. A light rustling, the ordinary touch of a piece of fabric, the smallest inflection of a voice, or a simple glance—these are received by the hysteric-phallus as constantly renewed sexual stimulations. Like a genital that wears itself out trying to respond to excitation but without ever discharging, the hysteric remains libidinally unbalanced; he is a body-phallus suffering from too much narcissism and no genitality. He experiences his sexuality everywhere in his body except in the very place where he should experience it. Penetrating a woman, for a hysterical man, or, for a woman, being penetrated, unconsciously means jeopardizing that part overinvested in fantasy, the phallus, an attack on which would lead to the complete disintegration of the body. A hysterical man surprised by his impotence at the moment when he is about to penetrate the desired woman, is, without knowing it, reactivating his unconscious fantasy from the time in childhood when he anxiously viewed his mother's castrated body, perceived as a desiring body and hence dangerous. Castration anxiety is here converted into sexual inhibition, which naturally results in dissatisfaction—dissatisfaction, it bears repeating, that protects him and to which he clings.

Figure 4–2 sums up the movement from the visual castration fantasy to hysterical conversion.

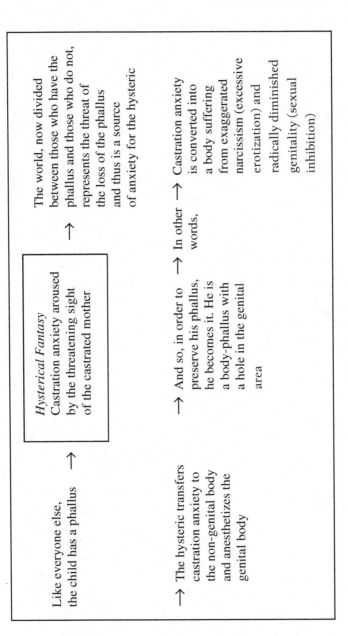

Figure 4–2. From the Visual Castration Fantasy to Hysterical Conversion

5

The Uterus in Hysteria:
A Fundamental Fantasy

> *The matrix or womb in women . . . is a living creature within them which longs to bear children. And if it is left unfertilized long beyond the normal time, it causes extreme unrest, strays about the body, blocks the channels of the breath and causes in consequence acute distress and disorders of all kinds.*
>
> Plato, *Timaeus*

Clinical practice demonstrates that the castration fantasy underlying hysteria is always accompanied by another fantasy, one so important that I call it *the fundamental fantasy in hysteria.* The scenario is very simple: a man and a woman, their bodies intertwined, conceive a child without any genital penetration. The hysteric is not only the creator and the actor in this dream, playing the role of the immaculate Virgin as well as that of the omnipotent Father; he is also, and above all, the place in which this divine procreative encounter occurs. Whether he embodies the bed, the house, or the soil of the earth on which the two mystical bodies take refuge, or whether he is the womb sheltering the fertile couple, the hysteric makes himself into the place that protects their sublime union. This is the basic fantasy that serves as a leitmotif pervading his existence.

In this fantasy there is one primary identification: the uterus, the organ that is the hollow womb containing the actual encounter in which life is generated. It is as though the hysteric identifies with the uterus in both of the forms that it assumes in his dreams. In the castration fantasy, it is the organ threatened with mutilation during sexual penetration, and, in the fundamental fantasy, it is the ideal receptacle that houses the meeting, felicitous and divine, of a man and a woman without genitalia. There are thus two types of uterus-phallus with which the hysteric identifies. Either he is the uterus as internal organ to be kept safe and never exposed, or he is the uterus assimilated to the hysterical body itself and considered to be a container enclosing two entwined bodies, those of a man and a woman with no genitalia. A uterus contained within a body, and at the same time a uterus containing two bodies—our thinking must be very supple if we are to understand these identifications of the hysteric, identifications that cross back and forth between an inside and an outside and awaken us to another kind of intuition, very different from the usual kind, a topological intuition.*

It is often said, and rightly so, that hysterics are bisexual. For indeed, in a universe where the difference between the sexes does not exist, they slip easily from the masculine role to the feminine, and vice versa. But we must go further and state that they are something other than bisexual: they are asexual, outside sex. Not only are they ignorant of sexual difference, they

---

*For further discussion of the topological relation between inside and outside, see Nasio 1987, pp. 197–202.

also embody the boundary, the neutral and external framework containing a procreative sexual union without penetration.

One further comment. Whether we view the hysteric as bisexual or outside sex, it remains the case that he does not know whether he is a man or a woman. What makes him a hysteric is that he has not managed to appropriate the sex of his body. In this sense, I part company with those who, following Charcot, claim that there is a masculine hysteria that differs from a feminine hysteria. I cannot assent to this view for the simple reason that the very problem of hysteria is the impossibility of psychically taking on a definite sex. The expression *masculine hysteria* is a contradiction in terms, since the noun *hysteria* means sexual uncertainty (neither man nor woman), while the adjective *masculine*, by way of contrast, makes a choice precisely where choice turns out to be impossible.

6

Differentiating Hysterical, Obsessional, and Phobic Fantasies

CASTRATION ANXIETY IS AT THE CENTER OF HYSTERICAL, OBSESSIONAL, AND PHOBIC FANTASIES

In order to bring my comments on hysteria into clearer focus, I must make a digression at this point. Just as we were able to recognize an original castration fantasy in hysteria, we can discern an unconscious foundational fantasy in obsessional neurosis and another in phobia. These latter fantasies are really only two derivatives of the hysterical fantasy that underlies all neuroses. The scenarios of the obsessional and phobic fantasies unfold, each in its own way, in accordance with the same drama of the castration ordeal, and—this above all—with the same anxious tension as in the hysterical fantasy. Let us look at these two scenarios.

The Obsessional Fantasy

The obsessional fantasy may be briefly summed up in the following scene:

A child, seized with incestuous desire for its mother, is overcome by anxiety (castration anxiety) when he hears the prohibiting voice of the father, the voice forbidding him to fulfill this desire under penalty of castration. The erogenous zone around which the obsessional fantasy is organized is that of hearing; it vibrates, suffers, and experiences pleasure as it hears the father's imperious voice.

Like all the fantasies I have been discussing, this scenario is unconscious, subject to the force of repression. Obsessional neurosis, the suffering that the obsessional subject undergoes consciously and in his symptoms, is the painful expression of the ego's struggle to repress, deny, and displace the castration anxiety contained in this fantasy.

The Phobic's Fantasy

The scenario of phobia is more complicated. In order to understand the following summary of the phobic fantasy, we should first recall that in this case castration anxiety is aroused essentially by the child's desire in regard to its father, not exclusively in regard to the mother as with obsessional and hysterical neuroses. It is the father who is at the center of phobia, first as object of a deadly desire (a patricidal desire), and then as object of a loving desire. The father is the leading character in phobia, even if, as in all neurosis, incestuous desire for the mother remains the point of departure.

Here, then, is the schematic summary of the sequence of events in the phobic fantasy:

Incestuous desire for the mother leads to the father's prohibition of the fulfillment of this desire. Hatred of the forbidding father (patricidal desire) arouses anxiety about punishment (castration). In order to moderate the anxiety, the child represses his hatred of the forbidding father. In place of the repressed hatred, there appears the opposite affect: love for the father.

Now, this love gives rise to another form of intolerable castration anxiety, *anxiety about showing love for the father in word or deed—fear of being dependent on the father, being too submissive, effeminized, that is, abused, even sodomized by the beloved father.*

The castration anxiety aroused by love for the father is rejected and is projected onto the external world. The anxiety thus cast outward fixes on an object in the surrounding world (a crowd, an enclosed space, a bridge, an animal, etc.); this object now becomes the threat that the phobic subject must flee in order to avoid being flooded by a conscious fear that is more tolerable than the unconscious castration anxiety.

If we were to select the culminating moment of the phobic fantasy from this sequence of events, it would be the point at which the child, struggling with the desire of filial love for the father, becomes anxious about being smothered by this beloved father. The erogenous zone around which the phobic fantasy is organized is not confined to a specific area of the body but extends throughout the muscle tissue. The erogenous zone in phobia comprises the muscles regulating the orifices by contracting or dilating them (relaxing or clenching the anus, the mouth, the eye, the digestive or respiratory system, etc.). What the phobic subject does is to place his castration anxiety out on the stage of the world in order to locate, control, and avoid it.[1]

We can organize the main points of the fantasies underlying the three primary neuroses as follows:

- In the *obsessional fantasy* the threat of castration enters through the ear, and the resulting anxiety, repressed and therefore unconscious, is displaced onto thought and becomes fixed on a neutral idea.
- In the *phobic fantasy* the threat of castration enters through all the orifices, tense or relaxed, of the body. The resulting anxiety, repressed and therefore unconscious, is projected into the external world and established and discovered there.
- In the *hysterical fantasy* the threat of castration enters through the eyes, and the resulting anxiety, here also repressed and therefore unconscious, is converted into suffering in the hysteric's sexual life. This takes the form of a general erotization of the body paradoxically accompanied by a localized inhibition in the genital area.

It is important to note that the castration fantasy I have identified as being the origin of neurosis is also the fantasy that all speaking beings,[2] neurotic or otherwise, must necessarily

---

1. On the problem of phobia see the abundant clinical material in Maillet 1988.

2. *Translator's note:* On the importance of language in Lacanian thought see Joël Dor, *Introduction to the Reading of Lacan, volume I: The Unconscious Structured Like a Language*, trans. Susan Fairfield.

encounter and overcome, and must encounter and overcome again and again. The characteristic feature of this fantasy in the case of the neuroses is the force with which it dominates the life of the subject, a life entirely organized around the castration anxiety that is at the heart of the fantasy.

*

*   *

Summary

We can sum up the fantasmatic origin of hysteria in a series of five propositions. But first I want to place particular emphasis on the third link of the sequence I am about to describe, the one that I consider to be the principal element.

I have been so insistent on castration fantasy as the cause of hysteria that the reader may have lost sight of the points made in the opening pages. The anxiety-arousing fantasy of castration that dominates the psychic life of the hysteric is to be sure the origin and the theme of neurotic suffering, but it is also (and primarily) a protective screen, a sure defense, against any possible approach of maximum pleasure. It is as though the hysteric would rather suffer from an anxious fantasy than confront what he fears as the absolute danger—experiencing pleasure. This, in my view, is the decisive factor in understanding the nature of hysteria and orienting the clinical listening of the psychoanalyst.

With this major point in mind, let us now sum up the five essential propositions:

- Experiencing pleasure is, for the hysteric, an ultimate, dangerous boundary that, once crossed, will inevitably cause him to sink into madness, to burst apart, and to dissolve into the void.
- Faced with the danger of pleasure, the hysteric mounts a stubborn refusal.
- To keep away from pleasure and to persist in his refusal, the hysteric unconsciously invents a protective fantasy, the anxiety-arousing fantasy of castration. In so doing, he creates a fictive threat of losing his phallic power in order to remain unaware of that other threat, likewise fictive but more obscure and indefinite, and much more terrifying—the threat of succumbing to pleasure. He becomes anxious about a castration he chooses to see as possible in order not to disappear before an unbearable pleasure. The refusal of pleasure is fantasmatically transformed into castration anxiety, where the threatened object is not the entire being but the phallus. In the chapter devoted to the psychoanalytic handling of hysteria we shall see that in clinical treatment the rejection of pleasure is expressed through the refusal to undergo the anxious ordeal of the castration fantasy.
- But while the fantasy rescues and protects the hysteric from pleasure, it plunges him into suffering in his body (somatic symptoms), his sexuality (the paradox of his sexual life), and his relationships (the desire for dissatisfaction). Castration anxiety is converted into bodily symptoms, sexual dysfunction, and the pain of discontent.
- The castration fantasy rescues and protects the hysteric from pleasure, but it disrupts the way in which he perceives the people he loves and those he hates. Like a distorting lens, the castration fantasy creates a neurotic

world in which strength and weakness are the sole deciding factors in love and hatred: I love or hate my partner according to my perception of his phallic strength or weakness. In this way, the hysteric's affective relations are inevitably transformed into relations of dominance and submission.

In sum, the logic of hysteria comes down to this: desire opens out onto pleasure, pleasure gives rise to the fantasy, the fantasy contains anxiety, and the anxiety, finally, is converted into suffering.

7

Imaginary Portraits of the Hysteric

Stretched out on the couch, the patient speaks. I listen, and a schema arises spontaneously in my mind, one that condenses three related factors: theoretical abstraction, transference desire, and the subject's history.

For indeed, as he listens to the patient, certain images impose themselves on the clinician. These are images conveying, in figurative form, the major elements of psychoanalytic theory that the practitioner may recognize in the course of his work. As dramatizations of theoretical propositions, such images prompt an analytic intervention that is, in general, appropriate and well timed. The analyst therefore makes use of these images to effect the transition from the abstract to the concrete as he puts forth his interpretation. It is as though, instead of wondering: "How should I intervene? What should I say to the patient?" he were to ask himself: "What should I fantasize? With what image, forged by theory but arising in the silence of my listening, should I work?" Let us ask precisely that question. What imaginary portraits begin to take shape in the analyst's mind as he actively listens to his hysterical patient or to the patient in the phase of transferential hysteria?

As we listen to a hysterical patient, in particular a man, let us imagine him to be a frightened little boy, huddled in a corner of the room, his eyes wide open as he covers his head with his hands as if to ward off the violence of some punishment.

Listening to a hysterical patient, in particular a woman, think of the father. Make the effort to imagine that this is not a woman who is speaking to you, but the father within her, a father who is in pain, his voice coming from a distance. The analyst's imagination can be active enough to give birth to this strange chimera composed of a little girl whose face, as he looks at it, has taken on the features of her father's face. A little girl whose genital area, like that of a porcelain doll, is just a smooth surface, marmoreal, without a crease.

If we now turn our attention to the bodily appearance of this woman patient, or to the gestures she makes with her hands, aren't these like the emanation in her of her father's living presence? His living presence even, and especially, if her father is dead or seems to be relegated to the background in her life?

As we listen to our patient, let us imagine that his body shelters a couple, a man and a woman with transparent bodies, entwined like two dream figures in an embrace without penetration or eroticism.

In listening to a hysterical patient, let us keep in mind that he is suffering from not knowing who he is, from not being able to stop, even for a moment, the unbearable procession of figures who inhabit him and under whose influence he cannot help offering himself to others.

In listening to a hysterical patient, let us imagine that his world—of which we are a part—is populated by strong and remote beings and by weak and pitiful beings. He pushes away the powerful ones, and yet he is on the lookout for their least frailty, their slightest suffering, their smallest weariness. He scornfully pushes away the powerless because they are made in his own image, and yet he summons them with the compassion of one who wants to bandage wounds.

*

*   *

THE ANALYST LISTENING TO THE PATIENT HAS A MENTAL REPRESENTATION OF THE CASTRATION FANTASY

With these imaginary portraits of the hysteric we have located ourselves in the psychic space of the analyst. But at this point a question arises: What do these images, cropping up spontaneously in the practitioner as he listens, have to do with the central scene of the castration fantasy? What role does the castration fantasy play in the concrete work of the analyst with his patients?

A word in advance. The scenes I have been describing in the preceding chapters, as I set forth the male and female castration fantasies, their obsessional and phobic variants, and the fantasy of the uterus, do not in any way correspond to events that actually occurred. The fantasy scenario of castration is not a real fact, and few of its details will be confirmed by, for example, the observable behavior of a child encountering the nakedness of an adult woman whom he loves. Nor does such a scenario correspond to the narrative imagery that a patient might present in a session; we rarely hear the account of such a fantasmatic sequence. But then where do we get this story of castration that is neither a real fact nor an account we have heard? It is important to be extremely clear here. The brief scenes that I have encapsulated like snapshots in this text are just abstract schemas of a fantasy scenario invented by the analyst to account for his clinical experience with hysterical patients and with neurotics in general. But are we dealing, then, with a whimsical reverie on the part of the analyst? With what justification does he—following Freud—construct such a fantasy, posit it as the basis of hysterical suffering, and state, as I have done, that this fantasy is the unconscious work of the subject himself?

The castration fantasy has a twofold legitimacy, both theoretical and practical. It is theoretically legitimate because the castration scenario as I have described it remains rigorously coherent with the entire conceptual edifice of psychoanalysis. Castration is one of the concepts most solidly based in theory. But its practical legitimacy is more important, because this scenario, though it may seem as stereotyped as an old-fashioned color print, recurs over and over again in an endless succession of imaginary variants in the course of treatment, an infinity of images that constantly prove, in our work with our patients, to be faithful expressions of the castration fantasy at the root of their suffering.

Now, concretely, what does it mean for the abstract schema of the castration scenario and its derivative images to be confirmed in our clinical work? First of all, when an analysand speaks to us and tells us about his conflicts and his complaints, we begin, of course, to understand the unconscious origin of his suffering from the vantage point of our place in the transference, but also by means of our mental representation of the fantasy schema offered to us by theory. There is no doubt about it: it is we analysts who, listening silently, imagine in the form of a scene the origin of the neurotic patient's suffering. Like a theoretical filter placed between the ear and the mouth of the analyst, between what he hears and what he says, the castration scenario proves to be a remarkable mental tool of his practice.

But two important reservations need to be stated. First, the imagined scene that we represent mentally to ourselves as the analysand speaks to us never reproduces in pure form the schema of the castration fantasy established by theory, but instead one of its infinite variants, the one peculiar to a given moment in the session. The second reservation is that the images in question are not contrived by the analyst; they present themselves spontaneously to him as he listens actively.

But how, then, does the analyst intervene on the basis of these images? When he breaks the silence of his listening, his intervention is to be considered a putting into words of the fantasmatic scene unfolding mentally within him, the scene that, in the form of images, expresses the unconscious origin of the suffering experienced by his patient. This putting into words, of course, is never a mere description of the details or the content of the imagined scene. The analyst silently keeps the image to himself and imparts to his patient only the words that convey the meaning of the scene. The sequence can be broken down into the following stages: an unconscious fantasy in the patient leads to suffering; listening to the patient's words in the session, the analyst sees the imagery of a scene arising spontaneously within himself, a scene expressing the castration fantasy, the cause of the patient's suffering; he performs a silent mental translation of the scene; and, finally, he communicates to the analysand the result of this internal process of translation. It is at this point that we await the analysand's reaction to our intervention, and when we receive it we are able in retrospect to confirm the value of the theoretical schema of the castration fantasy. It is, therefore, in the exercise of listening that we can validate this schema as a fertile fiction of analytic theory.

THE ANALYST LOOKS AT WHAT HE HEARS

To the multiple variants of psychoanalytic action—silence, explanatory interventions, and interpretation—we can, therefore, add a fourth factor: visual listening. It can be ascertained in clinical practice that certain interventions, as rare as interpretation, are actually linked to a transitory, elusive visual state experienced by the analyst. This is neither the silence preparing the way for an interpretative comment nor the reconstruction of elements of the patient's history leading to an explanatory intervention, but rather a highly distinctive subjective position on the part of the practitioner. His listening is so intensely focused on what the patient is saying that he not only forgets his ego but *looks at what he is listening to.* Let me try to describe this phenomenon of listening transformed into vision.

When the analyst perceives visually what he hears, we may take it that a special identification has occurred between the analyst himself and the auditory materiality of the words uttered by the patient. In order for the analyst to look at what he listens to, he has to have become the voice of the utterance he hears, and, even beyond this, he has to have become the physical sound of the spoken word. It is as if the person of the analyst were being displaced, like an erogenous object, through three bodily zones, the ear, the mouth, and the eyes. The sequence of this odd displacement is this: first, the analyst listens; then, as he listens, he forgets his ego; then he becomes the material sound of the spoken words; and, finally, he perceives visually the unconscious origin of what he hears.

In short, to look into the unconscious he has to have been what he hears. Looking at something, in this context, means becoming the object looked at. And so if he looks, in other words if he is what he sees, the analyst must have been what he hears. The process of transformation by which listening becomes a gaze is, of course, merely an explanatory artifice designed to aid in the understanding of an experience that in practice occurs in a condensed, compact manner. And my presentation of this artifice has another goal; in setting forth this sequence extending from listening to the gaze, I want to mark out the first stages of a theoretical research project that is worth pursuing.

In a paper devoted to transference (Nasio 1985), I defined interpretation as a return in the analyst of what had been repressed by the patient. The analyst's mental gaze may likewise be considered to be the return of the patient's repressed. Interpretation and gaze, then, are two modes of the return of the repressed, differing from one another insofar as the former is essentially a symbolic mode of return—interpretation consisting in a symbolic utterance—while the latter is essentially a fantasmatic mode. To be precise, I should say that when the analyst finds himself looking as he listens, he is fulfilling a unique desire, that of the analytic relation itself, or, to put it another way, that of the unconscious transference. In short, *the analyst looks at what the patient desires.*

8

Psychoanalytic Treatment of Hysteria and the Termination of Analysis

THE TREATMENT OF HYSTERIA CONSISTS IN GUIDING THE PATIENT TO EXPERIENCE SUCCESSFULLY THE ORDEAL OF CASTRATION ANXIETY

> *The hysteric is the splendid child who alone, at the threshold of the decisive ordeal, ready to cross it, says to us:*
>
> *I shall confront my anxiety by letting it pass over me, through me. And when, thanks to a word, a silence, or a cry, the anxiety has passed, I shall turn my inner gaze toward its wake, and there, where it has passed, there will be nothing more. Nothing but me when I have become the line of a scar, the surge of a new birth.*

Let us now turn to the psychoanalytic treatment of hysteria. I considered some aspects of this problem when, in discussing the conversion symptom, I defined the nature of the listening required of the psychoanalyst who is working with a hysterical patient. At this time I want to conceptualize the action of psychoanalysis differently, outlining the major event that must take place if the analysis is to free the neurotic of his suffering. Instead of going into the different technical aspects of the treatment of hysteria, I have chosen to focus exclusively on demonstrating how an analysand, whether hysterical or not, manages to overcome that other hysteria that is the analysis itself. For in fact the treatment reproduces the illness it is supposed to cure; analysis consists purely and simply of an artificial hysteria that patient and analyst must resolve together. It follows that the best way to understand the gist of the psychoanalytic treatment of hysteria is to examine closely the major event of the resolution of this transference hysteria.

At a moment well along in the treatment, at the height of the transference neurosis, the patient is faced with the choice of either consenting or refusing to undergo what I call the ordeal of castration anxiety. I want to make it clear that the analysand's engagement in one or the other of these alternatives, acceptance or refusal, is the result not of a conscious and deliberate choice but of an unconscious subjective state. This is a very distinctive state, the fruit of a long preparatory period during which the analyst and the patient himself have created the conditions in which the latter gets ever more intensely close to the final test. I call this the final test, not because it takes place during the last sessions (on the contrary, as we shall see, it occurs at the apogee of the analysis), but because what is at stake is so essential that the outcome of this ordeal will be decisive for the end of the treatment and the curing of the subject. If this passage is achieved, in other words, we may confidently expect that the treatment will go on to completion and the neurotic suffering will at last be alleviated. And so we can equate the ordeal of castration anxiety with the termination of analysis, understood not in the temporal sense, but as the decisive resolution of the transference neurosis. If the ordeal is not undergone, the transference neurosis is left hanging and the treatment remains uncompleted. Thus the manner in which the neurotic ends his analysis determines his cure. It is my conviction that analysis is just such a protracted effort culminating in the only experience that truly matters—the experience of anxiety. It is as though the entire course of the analysis were only a gradual preparation designed to arrive at this final point. What is this experience, this decisive ordeal? This chapter represents an attempt to reply to that question.

*

* *

DURING THE TREATMENT THE PATIENT SEPARATES TWICE: FIRST FROM HIMSELF, THEN FROM THE ANALYST

There are two types of separation. The first corresponds to the end of the analyst–patient relationship and takes place at the last session; the analytic relationship ends, even if the former patient happens to meet his analyst in various social or professional circumstances outside the analytic framework. The first separation, accordingly, is that of the final day, the farewell to the analytic relationship.[1] The other, very different separation also involves a detachment, but a special one that takes place in the endopsychic space of the analysand himself, both before and after the final session. This separation amounts to an autoseparation, a break with a part of oneself. Generated in the heart of the analysis, outside of time, it should be thought of not as a discrete event

1. On the problem of the end of analysis, see the excellent collection of papers in Colloquium 1988.

but as a long, slow, gradual unconscious process beginning with the experience of a painful ordeal at the culminating point of the analysis and continuing as a process of mourning that extends far beyond the last day on the couch.

You can see that, in differentiating two types of separation, I am making an implicit distinction between two registers of the treatment. The first register is the temporal one, in which the treatment advances chronologically in three phases that mark the development of the transference neurosis. There is an initial phase, in which the transference hysteria gradually establishes itself. The middle phase, characterized by a state of acute crisis in the analysand, represents the utmost exacerbation of the transference neurosis. It is at just this moment that the major event of the treatment occurs, the patient's encounter with the ordeal of anxiety. The third and final phase is the working through of the mourning and the process of autoseparation that result from the ordeal. This third phase is confirmed as such from the moment when analyst and patient agree to conclude, at some time in the near future, their mutual analytic work. This agreement can assume different forms, more or less explicit or tacit, direct or indirect.

The second register is that of the psychic process of the analysis. It unfolds in limitless time—limitless yet, as we shall see, cyclic—extending from the first embryo of the idea of consulting a psychoanalyst and continuing on beyond the analysis in another, unknown place. It is in this register that the autoseparation is inscribed.

Now, the way in which the patient takes leave of his analysis and his analyst is directly dependent on the ways in which he has undergone the singular ordeal and managed his autoseparation. If treatment is broken off abruptly or drags out endlessly in a state of impasse, we may reliably conclude that the ordeal was not successful, that the painful endopsychic process of separation, the autoseparation, has not occurred, and that as a result the analysis was not completed. This is, of course, a cut-and-dried, ideal formulation and should be considered a useful reference point for our clinical work, not an imperative law.

*
*   *

HYSTERIA IN THE TRANSFERENCE: CONDITIONS THAT LEAD THE PATIENT TO THE THRESHOLD OF THE ORDEAL OF ANXIETY

What is this ordeal that is so fundamental that, once it has been undergone, autoseparation takes place, the transference neurosis resolves, and the actual analytic relationship concludes in an entirely natural way? I have defined it elsewhere (Nasio 1989) as the painful transferential sequence. Lacan referred to it in various ways, sometimes as traversing the fantasy, on other occasions as getting beyond the level of identification. But before we look at this ordeal more closely, let us first recall the context in which it occurs.

What we are dealing with is, first and foremost, an experience of anxiety. Let me explain. My initial premise has already been established, namely that the neurotic suffering that led the hysterical patient to undertake analysis is the painful expression of a defense—repression and conversion—employed by the ego to contain the anxiety associated with the unconscious fantasy of castration. As we have seen, the mechanism of conversion, by means of which unbearable castration anxiety is transformed into the body-phallus, is an inefficient way to avoid anxiety. As a result of conversion the excess of anxiety can perhaps be diminished in the unconscious, but at the cost of being turned into another excess, that of the distressing erotization/inhibition of the body. Is there, then, some better way, something other than a defense, by which to foil anxiety? This is the question addressed in the psychoanalytic treatment of the neuroses, understood as the reactivation, via the transference, of the castration fantasy.

> What we are doing in an analysis is going back to the starting point, to the point of the fantasmatic origin of the neurosis, and reproducing at the very center of the treatment the same danger situation that gave rise to unconscious anxiety. In a word, we create anxiety in order to resolve it. We have to establish a new neurosis, a transference hysteria, and then try to find a better outcome than that of conversion. This other outcome, toward which the entire analytic task is oriented, can be summed up in the formula: *passing through anxiety*. The analyst's aim is to create the conditions in which the patient can finally come face to face with his fear.

In order to create these conditions, the analyst and the action of psychoanalysis must first induce a state of anxiety in the patient, thereby reactivating the anxiety that had previously been converted into the symptoms that brought the patient into treatment. The conditions under which the patient can confront his fear are those that govern the scenario of the castration fantasy, the scenario that the analyst, through his silence and his interventions, must re-create. They comprise three dangerous fictions, three threatening masks of the other that arouse anxiety, masks that the analyst must don: the castrated Other, the Other of the Law, and the Other of Perverse Desire.

The Castrated Other

This is the most threatening figure, one that we have located in the masculine castration fantasy underlying hysteria. It looms as a figure of horror when the child suddenly discovers the image of the naked, castrated body of the mother. The hole in the image is the danger signal perceived by frightened eyes. This lack, a dark shadow in a luminous body, means that one day I too may be mutilated. And yet, even as he is horrified and paralyzed by this threat, the child is, paradoxically, eager to let the danger retain its hold on him, to the point where he asks the other to show him the flaw of her castration and to frighten him. The castrated Other, for the neurotic, represents not only a menace that frightens, but also an appeal that seduces and reassures: "I'm afraid of your castrated body, and yet I ask you to show it to me, because your castration comforts me in my childhood as a phallic child." The castration fantasy is, to be sure, a source of anxiety, but let us not forget that it is, above all, a guarantee protecting the phallic child from that absolute danger, the danger of experiencing a boundless pleasure.

The Other of the Law

This is one of the paternal versions of the Other. Its function, which is to forbid incestuous desire and to punish it severely, is represented by the voice roaring out the Law of the incest taboo.

This is the major figure, resounding and dangerous, of the castration fantasy at the origin of obsessional neurosis. As was previously the case with the castrated Other, the child simultaneously flees and seeks the threatening presence that terrorizes and reassures. Once again the neurotic child, or, if you will, the phallic child, in effect says to the Other: "I'm afraid of the Law, but keep reminding me about it all the time. I ask you to command me, forbid me, and, if need be, to punish me."

The Other of Perverse Desire

This is also an eminently paternal figure, that of a father who takes his pleasure as he enjoys all women, a father who can abuse me, violate me, and take pleasure in my suffering. We have already met up with this third face of horror in discussing the phobic castration fantasy. I want to add here that, as in the two preceding cases, the same contradiction peculiar to neurosis recurs: the patient is anxious, but he would rather experience the horror and the anxiety of a frightened child than take on the difficult task of acknowledging his limits as a speaking and sexed being. Without ever looking his beloved father straight in the eye, he in effect asks him: "I am very afraid of you, but take me in your arms and make me the victim of your perverse desire."

Let me clear up a possible misunderstanding. This fantasmatic castration scene, like the two preceding ones, certainly brings perversion to mind. But make no mistake, this is only a dream of perversion; the neurotic is not a pervert, but someone who dreams of being one. The neurotic fantasy is merely the perverse fantasy of a subject who holds onto his anxiety and dreams of being an anxious child encountering a monstrously beautiful mother (the castrated Other), a terrifyingly protective father (the Other of the Law), and another father, perversely loving (the Other of perverse desire).

THE NEUROTIC'S DESIRE IS A DESIRE FOR ANXIETY

The analyst's problem, then, is that anxiety does indeed cause the patient to suffer, but, paradoxically, it comforts him as well. "I like to be afraid; it reassures me," as a patient once told me, describing in this way the bond that links every neurotic to his anxiety. This is a major obstacle to progress in treatment, for in order to undo the morbid dynamics of the neurosis, the clinician must first undo this extraordinary attachment of the patient to his anxiety. The analyst's most difficult task is at one and the same time to re-create a danger situation in the treatment, bring about a new anxiety in the patient, and get the patient to give up the anxiety with which he has been living all his life. But how to bring about this renunciation? Before turning to this issue, let us take a closer look at the way in which the hysteric links his being to his anxiety.

I have described the threefold fantasmatic threat: the hole in the image indicating mutilation, the voice of the Law announcing punishment, and the perversity of a desire that wants me to suffer. In such a situation, the subject believes not only that his phallus is at risk, but that his entire being might be annihilated. When he is seized by anxiety, the neurotic naturally reacts by converting it. In an attempt to get rid of it, he converts it into symptoms, and in an attempt to escape castration, he becomes the imaginary object that the other lacks. Whether he transforms castration anxiety into neurotic suffering or becomes, himself, the other's phallic object, far from ridding himself of his anxiety he becomes affixed to it. The hysterical solution to the problem of anxiety is therefore to love anxiety, to bind oneself to it body and soul to the point of becoming a thing—and this despite the distress of the symptoms. Hysterical conversion, which I at first conceptualized as a failure of repression, then as phallicization of the non-genital body accompanied by genital inhibition, now presents itself as the neurotic's irresistible fixation on his anxiety. The neurotic's desire is a desire for anxiety.

How, then, can we bring the patient to give it up? If he is to rid himself entirely of his anxiety, he must first encounter a new anxiety produced by the analysis and traverse it in order to leave it behind.

Let us sum up the analysand's situation before he undergoes the ordeal of anxiety. It is a danger situation consisting of the threefold menace of the hole, the Law, and perverse desire. We can condense these into the first, the threat of the hole. This leads to the arousal of anxiety: "I am anxious, and I have no recourse but to turn my anxiety into symptoms and to turn myself into the object that the other lacks; I become his object, and in so doing I fill in his hole and assure myself that the other remains castrated and fragile."[2] Having thus become the other's object, the subject finds his thought obliterated, his body petrified, and his narcissism pushed to the utmost. He experiences himself more than ever as an ego that takes pleasure in what it is, a fixated child. "In my anxiety, I am a motionless object that

---

2. This is why it is such a delicate task to treat a hysteric, who is always on the lookout for a flaw in the analyst. When he finally discovers one, he is disappointed and anxious about his analyst's loss of omnipotence, and at the same time he is reassured by the knowledge that the analyst is castrated after all.

no longer thinks and that experiences a voluptuousness that is just as much pain as it is narcissistic pleasure."

*

* *

THE ANALYST'S ACTION AIMS AT
RESOLVING TRANSFERENCE HYSTERIA

Faced with this anxious subject who enjoys his anxiety, what should the analyst do? How should he intervene so that his patient, the protagonist in the analytic scenario of the castration fantasy, can deal with his anxiety in some way other than by converting it into a narcissistic refuge? How can he resolve this transference hysteria? It must be said at the outset that most of the authors—beginning with Freud—who have studied the phenomenon of transference neurosis have not considered particular technical measures to diminish it. Freud is very cautious in view of the fact that overexact technical rules can lead to premature and inappropriate interventions. The analyst runs the risk of achieving a result contrary to the intended one by reinforcing the transference hysteria and prolonging the treatment to the point of condemning it to failure. When an analysis goes around in circles or loses its way, this is undoubtedly because the transference hysteria has not been resolved; that is, analyst and patient have not succeeded in opening up the path that would lead the latter to the threshold of the ordeal of castration.

It is clear that, considering what is at stake, any technical pointers would be out of place. Nevertheless the problem remains: How do we resolve transference hysteria? My answer will therefore be, not technical advice, but a suggestion that can orient the practitioner as he accompanies the analysand toward the ordeal of anxiety, making his passage easier. The analyst's interventions will first be aimed at finding the anxious child in the patient, the child who, cornered, confronts the insurmountable obstacle of the horror of castration. The impact of the action of analysis should be brought to bear just at the moment when the anxiety is about to be transformed into neurotic suffering and just before the subject identifies with the object. But what is this action? It is a changing of place. The analyst changes place because he has understood that the moment has come when he must modify his stance. He discards the masks of the Other of castration, steps aside, and establishes himself as symbolic witness to an ordeal that the subject *alone* can now undertake. I emphasize the word *alone* to evoke in the mind of the reader who is an analyst that almost moving moment when we sense that our patient is on the edge of the ordeal but we cannot push him into it.

The action of psychoanalysis occurs, then, at the precise moment when the patient hesitates to take the decisive step that would enable him to leave behind the life of a phallic child, the step that would usher him into the termination phase of treatment. The therapist must seize upon this instant in which anxiety arises, this moment when the subject finds himself confronted with a choice: either he can contain this burgeoning anxiety and make it his own, and this is the beginning of the ordeal, or he can convert the anxiety into suffering, and this is the unfortunate manner in which neurosis forms. In other words, he either agrees or refuses to undergo the ordeal.

It is in this sense that Freud (1937), at the end of "Analysis Terminable and Interminable," mentions the effects on the analytic work of the patient who unconsciously gives up the idea of undertaking the ordeal. For Freud, the refusal to expose oneself to anxiety often causes the treatment to be broken off abruptly. He explains this unwillingness to experience anxiety as a refusal of castration or, as he puts it, a refusal of femininity—yes, a refusal of femininity, for a man just as much as for a woman. Why equate the refusal of castration with the refusal of femininity? In the fantasy of a neurotic man, being castrated is the same as being a mere woman, a woman who, like all women in his fantasy, can only be submissive. Likewise, in the fantasy of a neurotic woman, not possessing the phallus that she demands is equivalent to being a dominated woman. Let us not forget that the universe of the neurotic is composed, not of men and women, but of omnipotent and castrated beings, the dominant and the humble. We can understand, therefore, that, quite apart from his anatomical sex, the neurotic assimilates the repellent image of himself as castrated to the image of a humiliated woman. Freud thus concludes that the refusal of femininity, or, as I would say, the refusal to undergo the ordeal, is a "No!" with which the anxious neurotic counters the fantasy of letting himself be castrated, in the case of the man, or the fantasy of not getting the coveted phallus, in the case of the woman. It is at this point that the patient breaks off the treatment violently and leaves the analyst in fury. Freud's description of this failure is well known: "We often have the impression that with the wish for a penis and the masculine protest we have penetrated through all the psychological strata and have reached bedrock, and that thus our activities are at an end" (1937, p. 252).

*
* *

PASSING THROUGH THE ORDEAL OF ANXIETY

The painful passage through the ordeal of anxiety is so fundamental that it is difficult to describe. Each of us at that moment,
when we think of our sessions as analysts or as analysands, will
have a unique representation. We can make use of theoretical
concepts, have recourse to allegories, or attempt formulations,
but the image of such an ordeal will remain incapable of trans-
mission, modeled on our personal history, on our analysis, and
on what we have learned from our patients.

I, for one, would imagine it as follows: approaching the
anxiety slowly until it is as close as possible, containing it in its
greatest tension, and crossing through it. Crossing it as one steps
through the frame of a doorway that, at the very instant of the
crossing, narrows into a thin, sharp blade that passes right
through the body, leaving there the umbilical trace of a transparent slit. Traversing anxiety means being traversed by it.

Let me try to express this in other terms. We pass through
anxiety when a word, an event, a gesture or a silence—it does
not matter—a dazzling revelation coming from the analyst or
welling up unexpectedly in me, the analysand, has made me
understand that I can accept loss, because what is at stake is not
everything, but only a part, a part that will be forever lost. I have
understood, not mentally but in actuality, that whatever the
final outcome of this passage through anxiety, the risk remains
necessarily partial and the loss is inevitably undergone. I have
understood, my body has understood, that I will never lose everything, and that if I gain, I will never gain without losing.

*
*   *

MOURNING AT THE TIME OF TERMINATION IS MOURNING NOT FOR MY ANALYST, BUT FOR A FICTION AND AN ANXIETY

The loss, then, is partial and inevitable. But what is this loss? It has many faces, but here, at the time of the ordeal of anxiety, it is above all the loss of an illusion, the illusion of an All (my phallus-being) and of the threatening monster who made me suffer (the castrated Other). Since I have understood that it is never the All that is in danger, that the risk is partial and the loss inevitable, I unveil the fiction of which I was the prisoner and, in unveiling it, I lose it. Yes, in accepting the loss of a part of myself, I lose the fictive omnipotence of the other and with it the very thing that was at stake—my supposed phallic power. And so my anxiety vanishes. Admittedly, though I am no longer anxious, I regret the disappearance of a fictive danger, of an infantile power (the phallus), and of an anxiety, now dispelled, that when all is said and done was only a safe way to exist.

It is here, in this painful but serene acknowledgment, that there begins the work of mourning the death of a transferential fiction, a task that will first end in the actual, concrete separation from the analyst and will then stretch into an endless process beyond the treatment. We can understand, therefore, that mourning a completed analysis is mourning a fiction and an anxiety.

Among the observable manifestations of this process of mourning, there is one unquestionable clinical sign observed by most analysts who have considered the problem of the end of the treatment. Starting with Ferenczi (1924/1968), who was the first to note it and did so in a striking way, and continuing up to the latest clinical studies of termination, all authors agree in acknowledging the same feature. The indisputable sign that marks the onset of the final phase of the treatment is that the patient, in a state of great serenity, has stopped waiting for love; that is, he no longer asks the Other, represented by his analytic partner, for assurance that he will receive that Other's love one day. For the analysand has understood that apart from the hope of getting out of the impasse in which he had been trapped, his analyst has given him nothing else. He has given him nothing else because he had nothing else to give except for this promise, this hope of getting to the portal of the ordeal of anxiety.[3]

There are still other clinical indicators of the termination phase. For example, during this time reminiscences of the beginning of the analysis often appear in the patient's narrative, details or words from the preliminary interviews, recollection of the date of the first appointment, the symptoms that brought the patient into treatment, and so forth. We also find dreams involving birth, or gestures of departure, train stations, conveyances such as planes or boats, people leaving and things arriving.

The end of analysis is not the removal of symptoms. When referring to the end of the analysis, people usually think of the removal of symptoms. Now, symptoms seem to have a life of their own, independent of the course of the analysis. Some of them disappear miraculously during the initial sessions, others change as the treatment continues—hysterical conversion can become phobic distress—and still others disappear or reappear long

---

3. According to the strict sense of the word "gift," I would claim that if there is something the analyst gives in an analysis, it is expectation. The analyst embodies the patient's hope of one day being in the most favorable position to undertake his passage and get rid of his neurosis. Now it is just this hope, or, as Freud (1905c) said, this trusting expectation on the part of the patient, that is the analyst's best therapeutic aid. If the subject is to have an opportunity to pass through the ordeal, he must have a firm hope of such a passage.

after the end of the analysis. The disappearance of symptoms should not lead the practitioner to imagine or expect that the end of the treatment is approaching. It is much more important for him to observe changes in the patient's subjective position. The patient is able to distance himself calmly from the analyst when he has stopped directing his demand for love to the Other of the transference neurosis.

The way in which the treatment ends attests to its productivity or failure. The manner in which treatment comes to an end is not decided after the analysis, but during and throughout it. Termination confers meaning retroactively on the whole of the analytic road that has been traveled. There is a concrete fact that the experienced practitioner can easily confirm: if a patient, after three years of apparently productive and eventful work, leaves the analysis and walks out slamming the door, the entire treatment will be called into question by this abrupt ending. Such a termination makes it clear beyond a doubt that the seemingly rich, fruitful analysis was not truly complete because the patient has not had the specific experience of leaving his neurosis. He leaves the analysis violently because he has not left his neurosis anxiously. We—analyst and patient—have not been able to create conjointly the conditions for the successful traversing of anxiety, and so the patient departs with his suffering intact. As I have said, the entire analytic trajectory converges on this essential passage and, beyond it, on the ultimate conclusion of the treatment.

Starting a new analysis: the problem of "segments." We can adopt this same perspective in considering the frequent cases in which patients undertake a second or third analysis some time after having finished the preceding one. This is the issue of "segments." When a patient decides to do a second piece of work in analysis, this is evidence, in my opinion, of the irresolution of his first experience. As the second analyst of a patient who, counting up his years on the couch, said to me: "I've had six years of analysis: four the first time and now two this time around," I did not hesitate to reply: "There aren't two analyses, or three, or five. There's only one analysis, the one we're in today, and we'll see later on whether it will turn out to be the kind of analysis we hope for, namely a completed analysis." I am convinced that the analyst must not work with the idea that his patient's second segment is the happy completion of the first. It would be more accurate to say that on the contrary, the current analysis is the only one in question. Why? Because the request to do a new piece of work clearly shows that the previous termination did not ratify an appropriate separation. Let me be clear. The cessation of analysis followed by a resumption indicates that the patient did not go through the process of autoseparation, that he did not succeed in separating from that part of himself that is his neurotic castration fantasy, and especially that he was not able to detach himself from the fictive figure of the Other and thereby give up his anxiety. Such a patient continues to uphold the existence of the Other of castration and to install the psychoanalyst, and psychoanalysis in general, in that place. And so when a patient decides to do a further piece of analytic work, we can safely say that the Other of his neurosis is still represented by one or the other of his successive analysts, that is, the place of the Other is still occupied by the analytic interlocutor.

For in fact, terminating an analysis involves my separating psychically from the analytic Other, my no longer addressing my demand for love to him, and my taking this demand outside the treatment. Being done with an analysis is being done with analysis in general, as if one were to say: "I've had it with analysis!" In the case of a second segment, then, the analysis was never terminated. In fact, the analysis does not yet even exist, since an incomplete analysis is one that has not yet come into being. A second segment, as I see it, is a new opportunity to establish the conditions for transference hysteria, to try again for the experience that did not take place—the passage through anxiety—and, finally, to conclude the analysis.

*
* *

PASSING THROUGH ANXIETY GIVES WAY TO THE PAIN OF MOURNING

Once the ordeal of anxiety has been traversed, there are three changes in the life of the analysand. First there is the pain of mourning, then the emergence of the subject of the unconscious, and finally a change in the patient's perception of his sexual identity.

When a hysteric undergoes the ordeal of anxiety, he separates from the phallic child that dwells in his unconscious. But such a separation is never a loss once and for all, since in the course of his life the patient loses and refinds the child of his fantasy many times over. The fact of having terminated an analysis and having successfully faced the ordeal of castration anxiety confers on the analysand one sole advantage, that of learning how to keep on losing and meeting up with his phallic child while being less affected, each time, by deep anxiety. Less affected by anxiety, but overcome by a new affect, pain, that now makes its presence felt, for neurotic anxiety disappears only to make way for the pain of mourning. What is this pain? How does it happen that the hysteric, like all neurotics, has been able to

exchange the permanence of anxiety for this pain that punctu-
ates and regulates the mourning for a part of himself? Why is
there mourning when the hysteric loses the phallic child of his
fantasy? And, more generally, why is there pain when we lose a
loved one? The answer is as follows.

THE PAIN OF MOURNING IS NOT THE PAIN OF LOSS, BUT THE PAIN OF FINDING WHAT ONE HAS LOST WHEN ONE KNOWS IT IS IRRETRIEVABLY LOST

The analysand has succeeded in passing through the ordeal of
anxiety and entering the final phase, the phase of mourning for
a part of himself that is the phallic child. Far from being over
and done with, this loss will recur many times throughout his
life, a life that is now understood to be a long and peaceful task
of mourning. My hypothesis is that pain arises whenever the
analysand meets, a thousand times, his phallic child, lost a thousand times. I want to stress that what hurts is not the fact of loss,
but instead the *refinding* of what we have already lost when we
know that we have lost it forever.

*

* *

To justify this hypothesis, we must return to Freud and
review briefly the train of thought that led to the belief that the
painful work of mourning is above all an endless series of encounters with the resurgence of the one who has disappeared,
and not with his absence.

The enigma that Freud attempted to clarify, one that is still current and challenging for us today, is this: Why do we feel pain when we lose a loved one? Like many of his answers, Freud's here is ambiguous and contradictory, correlating pain with the work of cathecting and decathecting the representations of the object one has loved and now lost. After reading his remarkable study of "Mourning and Melancholia" (1917 [1915]) and Abraham's work on the same topic (1924/1953), and especially in view of my own experience and that of my patients, I am convinced that the pain of mourning cannot be reduced to the emotion evoked by the loss of the loved one. We customarily attribute the pain to the separation, the tearing apart or the violence that a sudden loss entails. Thus, for some British analysts, the pain is due to the separation of the self from a part of itself. These authors' explanation of psychic pain centers around the idea of separation, an idea and a feeling that, admittedly, is shared by everyone who loses a loved one. Nevertheless I do not believe that pain results directly from separation, but instead that it appears when there is an *overinvestment* of the representation of the object that was loved and has now been lost. Freud speaks of cathexis and decathexis of the representations of the lost object, and it is my view that pain arises when we closely circumscribe and delimit, psychically, the representation of the lost object, when, from the ego's great abundance of unconscious representations, we select and isolate individually those of the lost loved one, concentrating our psychic energy on each of them. It is then, with each representation, that pain wells up.

What is it that we lose when someone dies? Essentially, what we lose is the imaginary framework that made it possible for us to love him. But this is not the loss that gives rise to the pain of mourning. Pain comes from meeting, a thousand and one times—as a thread is recognized in the countless knots on a weaving-loom—the representation of the loved one, but without the imaginary support that signified the other when he was alive. What is this imaginary support? It is my own image sent back by the living and loved other. Now that he is no longer there, I find his traces and his love, but without finding my own image. The work of mourning consists of my getting used to being in the silent presence of the lost other, but without the support of my images. In Lacanian terms: in mourning, I have to love the other without my ego-ideal, that is, without either the image of the other or my own image.

Lacan gives a very clear description of the state of a person in mourning in his Seminar on anxiety (1962–1963), observing that we mourn the person for whom we occupied the place of his lack. What this means is that at certain times and without my knowledge I occupied the place of the other's object of desire. This place is basically an emptiness that people or things can fill on occasion. Thus "to be in the place of his lack" means to be in the place of the lost person's object of desire.

Now, we mourn for a departed person only on two conditions: that this person served as an imaginary support for us, and that we occupied the place of the object of his desire. These are two intersecting planes, the imaginary plane of the reflection of images, and the level—let us call it fantasmatic—on which one of the partners occupies the place of the object of desire. In a so-called love relationship the partners are located, each in his own way, on one or the other of these planes. So we can paraphrase Lacan's formulation by saying that we are in mourning for someone who mattered for us (which we knew) and for whom we were the fantasmatic object of desire (which we didn't know). What Lacan's statement ultimately means, then, is that in order for there to be mourning for someone, there needs to have been a twofold relationship to that person, consisting of love and fantasy.

Mourning cannot be completed if there is insufficient time and an absence of ritual. Ritual involves the time necessary for taking up the representation of the lost object, overinvesting it, and finally separating from it little by little. Ritual takes place over time, and an incomplete mourning process has not allowed for enough time. This is the case of Hamlet, when his father is buried in a hurry with no funeral rites, with no provision for the psychic time that is essential for coming to terms with the fact that the other is no longer there.

*

*   *

This digression on the pain of mourning was intended to make it easier to understand that, at the end of an analysis, what hurts for the patient who has lost the child of his fantasy is not that he has lost it, but that he meets up with it again when he knows it has been irretrievably lost. Passing through anxiety has thus given way to the pain of mourning (see Figure 8–1).

PASSING THROUGH ANXIETY IS FINDING THE BIRTHPLACE OF THE PERSON I HAVE BEEN ALL ALONG

We must pass from beginning to beginning. And that is life.

The most important consequence of the traversal of anxiety is the coming into being of the analysand as a subject. When the ordeal has been accomplished, his voice says to us:

ANXIETY before the ordeal	PAIN OF MOURNING after the ordeal
Anxiety arises in the face of the threat of losing everything.	Pain appears after the loss of a fiction. This pain stems not from the loss, but from finding the lost fiction when we know that it is irretrievably lost.
Cannot be assimilated	Can be assimilated
The anxiety is converted into suffering.	The pain is not converted.
When converted, anxiety obliterates thought, petrifies the body, and reinforces an exaggerated narcissism in the subject.	The pain heightens endopsychic perception, reveals truth, and opens onto a serene sadness.

Figure 8–1. Comparison of the anxiety preceding the ordeal and the pain of mourning after traversal of the ordeal

I have understood that I shall never lose everything and that inevitably I shall lose a part of myself. And, because I understand that, I have lost my fiction. But what is left? Nothing; there is nothing left of the fictive totality, of the fantasmatic danger and the anxiety. Only I am left. Who is this I? The subject, I mean the only absolute, unique subject, the subject of the unconscious, who I have never stopped being because he was already there beforehand, unbeknownst to me. I have understood in actuality, and through my understanding I have refound the person I already was without knowing it.

Where that was, I have come to be. Freud's celebrated maxim, as reinterpreted by Lacan,[4] echoes the eternal oracle of Parmenides: "For me, the beginning is coherent with the end, for it is there that I shall come back again."[5] In the constitution of the subject, too, the end and the beginning of the analysis coincide; in the treatment there is no future, since going forward is in fact a return, not to the past but to what is most inaugural and authentic in me.

----

4. *Translator's note:* The formula under discussion is *Wo Es war, soll Ich werden*, translated in the *Standard Edition* as "Where the id was, there the ego shall be" (Freud 1933, p. 80). Since the German *das Es* and *das Ich* are, literally, "the it" and "the I," a more accurate translation would be "Where 'It' was, 'I' must come to be." Lacan's reworking of the maxim is facilitated by the closeness in tone of the French *le ça* (the 'that') and *le je* or *le moi* ('the I' or 'the me') to the German *das Es* and *das Ich* and is based on his theories of the unconscious and of subjectivity. For Lacan's account of the Freudian formula in the context of his own thought, see Lacan 1977a, pp. 128f. and 299f.

5. Parmenides, Fragment 5, in Tarán 1965. *Translator's note:* The meaning of the original Greek text is controversial. I have not followed Tarán's reading but have translated the passage in a way that brings it closer to Dr. Nasio's intention.

The course of an analysis forms a trajectory with two turns that link, in a spiral, the final point and the beginning of a cyclic and indeterminate process that is always open-ended. I have been speaking of the treatment in terms of two temporal registers, one actual and chronological, the other psychic and logical. We can now see that these two registers complement one another and describe a general movement of the analysis in a boundless, cyclical time. (This conception of time is close to that of the Neo-Platonist philosopher Plotinus.)

What, exactly, is this open and limitless cycle of an analytic treatment? It comprises two circular turns that do not close but describe a spiral, and three particular moments: the initial interview (M1), the ordeal of anxiety (M2), and the birth of the subject (M3), as shown in Figure 8–2.

The first loop begins with the initial interview (M1) and ends with the ordeal of anxiety (M2). These two time periods overlap, since in the initial interview the analysand recounts his suffering and in the ordeal of anxiety he passes through the fantasy at the origin of this suffering.

The second loop is also open-ended. The circuit begins with the successful outcome of the ordeal (M2) and ends with the emergence of the absolute subject (M3) whom the analysand had always carried within himself and whom the passage through anxiety only had to reveal. This revelation occurs not all at once but in an endless series of events. These two time periods also overlap, since the success of the passage means that the patient has released himself from his neurosis and has finally found the true subject he has been all along. Now that the analysis is over, he is awaited by this subject who, without knowing it, he already was and who he now becomes. That is so because it was already so: such is the ineluctable law of the unconscious.

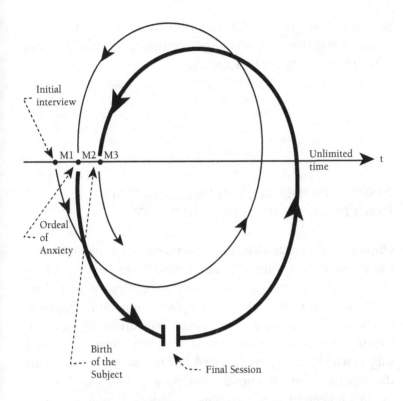

Figure 8–2. Diagram of the Duration of an Analysis

Analysis as a treatment is of limited duration. But analysis as a psychic process has a cyclic and unlimited duration.

We can schematize the four stages of the analytic cycle as follows: the imperceptible subject of the unconscious → the neurotic ego → traversal of the ordeal of anxiety → encounter with the imperceptible subject of the unconscious. It is clear that the time required for an analysis is not, strictly speaking, its linear and temporal duration—three years, five years, and so on—

but instead the time of a difficult ordeal and of a remarkable and repeated revelation. Analytic time contracts into the moment when truth emerges into actuality.

*
*   *

PASSING THROUGH ANXIETY CHANGES MY PERCEPTION OF MY SEXUAL IDENTITY

Once the ordeal of anxiety has been traversed, mourning begun, and the analysis terminated, what happens? The analysand, now alone, works through his mourning and enters the period we call *post-analytic*. But what is taking place within him? What scar has been left by the experience of autoseparation? Or again, in Lacan's terms, what is the new state of the unconscious of a subject who has completed his analysis? It is an unconscious plus the experience of the unconscious, he might answer. I would say that it is an unconscious plus the ordeal of anxiety. It is an unconscious that has been altered, made more supple by the traversing of a painful passage, an unconscious more flexible in its ability to perform unconscious self-perception, or, as Freud calls it, endopsychic perception.

Now that anxiety has, as it were, passed through me, I am now aware endopsychically of my limits as a speaking and sexed being. What does this mean; what has changed in the unconscious? The nature of my perception of my own sexual identity has changed. Before the ordeal, the subject was unaware of— had repressed—the difference between the sexes, and he perceived the lack of a phallus as the lack of an absolute All with absolute power. And afterwards? Will he finally recognize that there is a difference between the sexes, that there are men who are men and women who are women? He will do better than that. He will do something other than acknowledge the existence of sexual difference: he will be able to interrogate it. He will neither be unaware of sexual difference, after the ordeal, nor will he set it up as incontestable dogma. It will be neither repressed nor dogmatized, but acknowledged and immediately put in question. Altered by the passage, his perception will no longer be sucked outward by the environment but turned inward, back toward him. Before the ordeal, his awareness, oriented toward the exterior, was on the lookout for signs of the Other's castration, interpreted as the lack of an All; afterwards, turned inward, it takes hold of the enigma of the sexed being.

9

Brief Observations

We must not be led astray by the seductive charm of the hysteric. The hysteric is not a seducer; he is a fearful being.

*

There are three situations in which the hysteric is at peace and allows himself a respite: when he is in love, when he is sad, and (in the case of a woman) when she is pregnant.

*

The hysteric has a twofold passion, love and hatred. When he loves, he loves his partner with the exception of his genital; when he hates, he hates the genital of his partner, detached from the partner's beloved person. This love and this hate, always passionate, intersect and alternate ad infinitum. It often happens that love is transformed into devotion to a sexless other (an invalid, a priest, or a psychoanalyst). And sometimes hate is transformed into a violent wish to tear away the other's genital (devouring, fellatio).

*

The sensual appearance and behavior of hysterics gives the impression of a strong sexual desire. But once one gets past this charm, the sexual life of hysterics is disturbed, limited, and fundamentally unsatisfying.

*

The hysteric experiences his sexuality in three different ways. He suffers in his body, because symptomatic suffering is the psychic equivalent of orgasmic satisfaction. He masturbates, because masturbatory pleasure is preferable to the danger of the sexual relation. And he is split between dazzling hypersexuality and the painful reality of suffering experienced as genital anesthesia.

*

The hysterical attack translates into the language of a body suffering erotic pantomimes that have never existed except in daydreams.

*

In hysterical blindness the subject has lost sight of the image of the other and focuses his unconscious gaze on one sole thing: the other's libidinal charm. He loses his sight but preserves the intensity of his gaze.

*

But the libidinal charm of the other is perceived by the hysteric not as a sexual characteristic, but as a sign of strength or weakness. What excites a hysteric is not the other's sexuality but the vulnerability of his strength or the possibility of remedying his weakness.

*

Can it be that one of the privileged sites of hysteria in our time is psychoanalysis itself? For what is psychoanalysis if not the reproduction of hysteria in order to cure hysteria? Lacan and Freud describe the analytic process as a directed paranoia; I would add that it is also a directed hysteria.

*

The hysteric says, in effect: "To avert the danger of plea- sure in the sexual relation, I insist on having two guarantees— that the Other suffer from impotence, and that he forbid me to have pleasure." In other words, in order to avoid pleasure the neurotic transforms the Other into an impotent prohibitor.

*

READING THE LACANIAN FORMULA FOR THE HYSTERICAL FANTASY

Lacan (1960–1961) has reduced to a formula the essential move- ment of the hysterical castration fantasy: $\frac{(o)}{-\varphi} \Diamond O$

We can read it in this way: the hysteric looks at ($\lhd$) the castrated Other (O), becomes anxious, and, in the face of this anxiety, identifies with the imaginary object that the Other lacks ($-\varphi$). The ($-\varphi$) thus becomes the ($+\varphi$) embodied by the hysteri- cal ego. The ego is ($+\varphi$) with the exception of the genital area, which remains anesthetized ($-\varphi$). The result of this conversion, which the hysteric thought would save him, is the pain of dis- satisfaction (o), to which the subject is eventually reduced. In other words,

is equivalent to

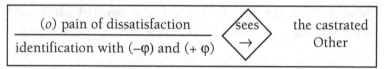

which is equivalent to

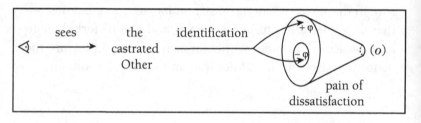

*

THE LIBIDINAL PRESENCE OF HYSTERIA: A CLINICAL EXAMPLE

I lie down on the couch and something goes away; words go away, language disappears and feeling appears. When I'm here, I see myself as if I were in a cloud, I feel self-hypnotized as if I were under the influence of a hypnosis that I myself brought on. I lie down, I feel very dependent on everything, on you and on what happens to me. And then little by little I know that I can make decisions about my emotions and feel what I want to feel. I lie down and all of a sudden I begin to feel, and to want to feel even more. I wait for feelings, not only in my body but also in my head. As if there were a body in my head and feeling went down from my head into my physical body. I know that when I feel the dropping of this feeling that's going down it will turn into an orgasm.

I'm very embarrassed, because I don't want to have forbidden feelings here. I'm waiting for the feeling to drop down and flow into my body, but for it to stop just short of orgasm. I don't want to have sexual pleasure here in the sessions, but I want to experience everything up to that point.

*

EXAMPLE OF A FEMININE FANTASY OF HYSTERICAL ANXIETY AND HATRED OF THE MOTHER-PHALLUS

Everything I offered as a little girl ran the risk of being destroyed by my mother. She wanted me to be dead, to go away, to kill myself. But I don't want to kill myself, because that would give her too much pleasure. Yes, I hate her; I won't commit suicide in order not to gratify her desire to see me dead. I'd really like to kill her and to get up all my strength to make her disappear. I have a problem with masculine and feminine, because I'm a woman but I'd also like to be a man who could cope with the destructiveness coming from my mother. My father never counted for anything at home and never stood up for me. No, it was just me; I was the man who dared to go against my mother.

10

Questions and Answers on Hysteria[1]

You consider hysteria to be the basis of the neuroses, whereas other authors see it as the "healthiest" neurosis. What is your thinking here?

ALL HYSTERIA CONCEALS A KERNEL OF SADNESS

To be sure, certain classical analysts consider hysteria to be the most mature neurosis, because from the point of view of the development of the libido it is the one that comes closest to the final phase, the so-called genital phase. The principal advocate of this position is Karl Abraham, for whom hysteria, as a fixation at the phallic stage, the stage immediately preceding the attainment of genitality, is the most evolved neurosis. Yet clini-

---

1. These questions are based on those that have followed various oral presentations on the topic of hysteria.

cal experience reveals that on the contrary hysteria should be considered the most elementary on the scale of the neuroses, the one on which obsessional and phobic structures are built. This is not only my position, but also that of Lacan and of Melanie Klein. It was Lacan (1970–1971) who, after he made hysteria the paradigm of the neuroses, established *hysterical discourse* as the structure governing every neurosis, or, to be more exact, every neurotic bond. And then there is the way in which hysteria is related to psychosis itself, in particular to melancholia and schizophrenia. In Kleinian theory, for example, hysteria is seen as a defensive rampart against a melancholic psychotic core (compare the theoretical positions of Eric Brenman and Herbert Rosenfeld in Laplanche 1974). For the Kleinian analyst, a hysterical patient is first and foremost a potential melancholic. I cannot deny this view, so often confirmed by clinical experience, but on the other hand I would not employ the same concepts in thinking about the relationship of hysteria to melancholia. I have used other terms in this study to emphasize how very close the hysterical identification with pain is to the psychotic abyss of melancholia.

*
* *

Are certain people especially predisposed to hysteria?

WE ARE ALL HYSTERICS!

I would answer, first of all, that at our own times and in very different ways we are all neurotics, since we all have to confront the fantasy of castration and to do so indefinitely. The experience of castration recurs constantly throughout life, and we are vulnerable to hysteria—and phobia and obsessionality—every day. I agree with Moebius (1888), a famous psychiatrist contemporary with Freud; wishing to broaden the concept of hysteria, he proclaimed that we are all hysterics.

That having been said, I must admit that some people have an easy time of the ordeal of castration, while others become fixated there and wear themselves out. But to return to your question, I'd like to remind you that Freud considered the predisposition to neurosis to be an unsolved riddle. His friend Breuer, however, had constructed an etiological theory of hysteria based on a particular ego state that renders the subject more likely to experience trauma and become hysterical. Breuer believed that bringing on a trauma that would lead to hysteria required not only the local impact of the traumatic shock, but also a psychic predisposition on the part of an ego with a weak level of consciousness. Since such a twilight state, very vulnerable to attack, could be produced artificially under hypnosis, Breuer called it a *hypnoid state* and considered it to be the principal cause of hysteria (Breuer and Freud 1893).

*
*   *

Could you go into more detail on why there is no feminine hysteria different from a masculine hysteria?

Before answering, I'd like to note that this study on hysteria is clearly influenced by my work as an analyst. After all, in order to put forth hypotheses such as those I've been offering, you have to be in the consulting room, to have been analyzed, to sit in the analyst's chair and yield to the experience of listening. Then it is clear that, at one time or another during the treatment, certain patients in their own way adopt what I call a hysterical position, a position that can be assumed by a man as well as by a woman, with no specific difference. The hysterical position cannot be reduced to the man/woman duality, and so I think it's a mistake to do as Charcot did, and some modern authors still do, and study an entity they call "masculine hysteria." Both theory and practice argue against distinguishing between masculine and feminine hysteria.

To maintain such a split is to ignore the fact that, as we have seen, hysteria embodies the suffering of someone who is indeterminate as far as sexual identity is concerned. The hysteric suffers from not knowing whether he is a man or a woman. He cannot call himself one or the other because he remains on the threshold of the experience of castration anxiety. In other words, he is fixated on the fantasy in which the world is not divided up into sexed men and women, the former with a penis, the latter with a vagina, but is split into those who possess the phallus and those who are deprived of it. The hysteric's world is an infantile one composed of the powerful and the powerless, the strong and the weak, the young and the old, the athletes and the handicapped. He suffers because he is in the wrong play: his drama unfolds in a child's fantasmatic reality where the man/woman distinction does not exist, and yet he lives out this drama in a world in which sexed reality is problematical, to be sure, but unavoidable.

We could, of course, call hysteria masculine, hysteria affecting someone who is anatomically a man. But this classification would be a serious misconstrual of the way in which the hysteric suffers from not knowing whether he is a man or a woman, from

QUESTIONS AND ANSWERS ON HYSTERIA **115**

repressing sexual difference to the point of being unaware of it. What actually is the hysteric's desire? Following Lacan, we know that it is a desire for dissatisfaction—but in what sense? Not only the dissatisfaction that the hysteric experiences and in which he so stubbornly basks, but also the dissatisfaction that pertains to the man–woman relationship. The hysteric's desire is to determine the precise degree of a man's dissatisfaction with the woman he loves, or a woman's with regard to the beloved man. He always tends to establish himself at the center of a couple, the place where the man–woman bond is weak because they are sexed and speaking beings. But we also have to understand that the hysteric suffers from his sexual indeterminacy even as he preserves it as a necessary and reassuring ambiguity. In other words, the hysteric would rather not know about his sex, and suffer from this ignorance, than undergo the painful ordeal of castration that would enable him, not to be a man or a woman, but to endure the enigma of the man's and the woman's sex.

*

*   *

Why are there more female than male hysterics?

This is an old question, one that psychiatrists, ethnologists, and psychoanalysts have wondered about but have never been able to answer decisively. I'll attempt a response from the psychoanalytic point of view, keeping in mind that the problem is one that has been dealt with, at length and often in a striking way, in the realm of ethnopsychiatry. Is it only in our western, Judaeo–Christian culture that hysteria and femininity seem to go together? What happens in other contemporary civilizations?

Or, within our own cultural context, what has been the influence of female figures in the Christian religion—Eve, Mary, Mary Magdalene, and so forth, all model hysterics—on this obvious social fact? These are interesting and legitimate questions, deserving of serious study.

But as far as a psychoanalytic response is concerned, I'd like to begin by recalling an important theoretical proposition that I've already discussed, namely that the hysteric suffers in the way he does because he remains frozen in the position of the object loved, cherished, and desired by the Other of his unconscious fantasies. Now, if there is someone who must normally and necessarily pass through this stage of being the Other's object, it is certainly the woman. Indeed, according to Freudian theory, the woman must go through identification with the father's object, that is, with the phallus. In order to tolerate the admission that she has been castrated and find a solution to her penis envy, the little girl identifies with the father's penis, or, to be more accurate, with his phallus. Since she does not have this coveted object, she becomes it; she turns herself into the paternal phallus. Let me hasten to note two reservations. First, the identification with the paternal phallic object can easily vary, developing into an identification with different traits of the father himself. And, second, this identification never remains fixed. The little girl, as she grows into womanhood, goes through a temporary masculine phase for several years; she acts like a boy as a way of being the paternal phallus. This phase, theoretically, lasts until puberty, at which time the femininity of the adolescent girl finally blossoms.

And what about the hysteric? Why are there more women than men among them? Or, rather, why is hysteria always marked by femininity? Well, because every hysterical neurotic, man or woman, has resorted to the same identification with the phallus of the paternal Other that the woman performs in the normal course of her development. But with this essential difference: when a woman becomes feminine she recognizes, not without pain, that her genital remains an enigma, but that it is neither the phallus nor the absence of a phallus. The hysteric, on the other hand, is still anchored in the neurotic and painful identification with the phallus. We can now see that more women than men are hysterical because the woman is always more susceptible than the man to becoming fixated in the phallic identification.

*
*   *

Could you be more precise about the object with which the hysteric identifies?

THE HYSTERIC'S IDENTIFICATION

The ego of the hysteric identifies with the image of the other considered solely as a sexed being, or, more exactly, with the genital region of the other. Abraham (1924/1953) speaks of the imaginary place of the other's genital, heavily invested by hysterical patients to the detriment of the rest of the image of the person. It is as if the hysterical subject focused and flung his whole ego onto the genital center of the image of the Other, discounting the remainder of the image. It is precisely this identification of the hysterical ego with the Other's genital organs that I have discussed in terms of the subject's identification with the phallus that is lacking in the castrated other. However, Abraham also recognized the opposite possibility, in which the hysteric identifies with the image of the entire person but without the genitals, as if, in the genital area, the image were covered by an opaque white patch. Abraham describes this double mode of partial identification in commenting on a hysterical patient's relationship with her father. Unable to see her father as a whole, this patient had a compulsive interest only in his penis. She identified both with the father and with the genital organs that represented him.

To illustrate further this double identification with the image of the other, let us briefly consider Dora, Freud's (1905a [1901]) hysterical patient. Here we can see vividly how Dora identifies either with the image of the other reduced solely to the genital area, in which case the other is perceived as sexually *desirable* thing, or with the image of the other minus the genital area, in which case the other is perceived as sexually *desirous* insofar as, having a hole in him, he desires to fill in his lack.

Recall the intensity with which Dora is able to assume both of the complementary roles played by Mrs. K. (the desirable one) and her father (the desiring one) on the stage of her own hysterical fantasy. First there is the role in which Mrs. K. is a sexually desirable object for the father, reduced to the sole dimension of a thing sexually desirable by a male lover.[2] But, conversely, Dora can also play the role of the desirer who is the one with the lack;

---

2. This sexually desirable thing that Mrs. K. becomes is what psychoanalysis calls the *phallus*. In Lacanian theory the complete term would be *imaginary phallus*, imaginary because this thing to which Mrs. K. is reduced is the sexual place—the genital region—perceived in the image of the other: "the phallus, that is, the image of the penis, is made negative in its place in the specular image [of the other]" (Lacan 1977a, p. 319; translation modified).

she then identifies with her father who desires a woman. It is important to note that the impetus of this movement toward identification with the desirer is marked by the fundamental tendency of the hysterical ego to identify with a desirer who not only seeks but takes pleasure in seeking, a pure desirer who takes pleasure in being in the state of desire. And so the immediate identification of Dora with her desirous father is part of a line stretching toward the abstract horizon where, finally, she may find the enigmatic essence of femininity. Dora hopes, then, to go beyond all limits in joining a Mrs. K. fantasized, this time, not as a desirable thing, but as borne by the most lofty desire, the mysterious feminine desire, pure desire without an object.

But there is still a third modality of hysterical identification. This variant is somewhat unacceptable to thought yet clinically significant. The hysterical ego identifies not only with the particular image of the other, for example, with Mrs. K. as sexually desirable object or with the father who desires the lady, but also with the emotion of the orgasm fantasized by Dora as part of the embrace of a man and a woman. Freud (1909) was prepared to equate the hysterical fit with an orgasm. When you see a hysteric fainting, he said decisively, you can be sure that he is doing more than having an orgasm; he is identifying with the sexual agitation shared by the members of the fantasized couple. As surprising as it may seem, we must conclude that the hysterical ego is completely assimilated to the couple's sexual turmoil. This state of agitation is, fundamentally, the couple's dissatisfaction, since in the hysteric's fantasy the sexual encounter is always a failure.

Within a single clinical entity, hysteria, we thus find three varieties of the identification of the ego with an aspect of the other. No other clinical structure includes such a multiplicity of partial identifications, mutually exclusive and yet complementary. When all is said and done, hysteria consists in the assumption, one by one, of all the places in the sexual parade, all the positions relating to desire. Every hysterical dream, symptom, or fantasy condenses and actualizes a triple identification: identification with the desired other, the desiring other, and the discontent of the two lovers. We might even add a last identification typical of hysteria, the identification with a third party who brings together the couple or separates it. The reply to the general question about the nature of the object with which the hysteric identifies would therefore be that the object of identification is not the beloved woman,[3] or the loving man, or even their shared sexual dissatisfaction, and not the third party offstage, but all of these together. In a word, the hysteric essentially identifies not with a specific object, but with the *link* that joins one of the partners in the fantasized couple to the other.

MATERNITY AND HYSTERIA

And I want to stress that there is yet a fifth kind of hysterical identification. For the hysteric identifies with the man, the woman, the third party excluded from their encounter, and with the pain that separates them, but above all—the final identification—with the space that brings together and contains the couple. In the life of a hysteric a basic fantasy always stands out against the horizon: "I am not the man, or the woman, or the pain of their bond, but this earth that has welcomed their

---

3. We can understand why it is mistaken to believe that hysterical desire is homosexual.

divine encounter, an encounter without carnal exchange of which I am nevertheless the fruit." This fifth identification corresponds to the fantasy in which the hysterical subject serves as a crucible sheltering and protecting the divine coupling of two sexless bodies. This fantasy has led me to consider the final hysterical identification as being with the uterus, a hollow organ in which germinal cells are fertilized without having been produced by a sexed body. It is as though for the hysteric, as for Plato, the uterus were a migratory organ, a mobile phallus wandering about in his fantasy world; from an internal organ threatened by penetration, it turns into the external container that embraces two immaculate bodies. Plato's remarkable comment about the uterus as a thirsty animal wandering in a woman's body in search of a contents that will fill and satisfy it touches on the central point of our clinical work with hysterical patients. This point has to do with maternity. For how often have we noticed the decrease in hysterical suffering during the last months of a hysterical patient's pregnancy? Maternity is, as it were, a possible alternative way of undergoing the ordeal of castration: the uterus is no longer a phallus threatened and adrift; it is now that other figure of the phallus that is the child about to be born.

*
* *

I understand the connection you make between the refusal of castration and the refusal of femininity in the neurotic, but what about femininity in a neurotic man who has passed through the ordeal of anxiety?

THE FEMININITY OF THE FATHER

Your question is important because it concerns a man's relation to femininity and the paternal function (Nasio 1990b). If the neurotic takes a risk and undergoes the ordeal of anxiety, the femininity that he had rejected with horror—femininity incarnated by the image of a castrated and humiliated woman—is transformed into another femininity, his own, what we can call the feminine part of a man. My hypothesis is this: I believe that the man who is called upon to be a father must recognize the feminine part of himself. In fact, the man who acknowledges with pain his feminine aspect is better able to assume the difficult role of father than the man who does not acknowledge it. Why? Recall the definition of neurosis. One way to characterize neurotic suffering would be to state that the neurotic is someone who, because of anxiety, rejects his femininity, that is, refuses to yield to the Other lest he be abused, penetrated, or raped. For a neurotic, as we have seen, femininity is synonymous with passivity and submission. To be a woman is to have the experience of the woman in his fantasies, who suffers as a result of her castration. The woman of the neurotic fantasy is someone who is castrated, submissive, always vulnerable to an Other's perverse action—specifically, to the action of a perverse and tyrannical father. I want to emphasize that the neurotic's idea of femininity is wholly a product of his anxious castration fantasies and that this idea has nothing to do with the psychoanalytic conception of femininity. I am dwelling on this point because there is a huge misunderstanding between psychoanalysis and certain currents of thought—often feminist—that equate neurotic fantasy and analytic theory and therefore reproach psychoanalysts for entertaining the neurotic idea of the castrated and therefore submissive woman.

I won't take the time to expand on this comment here, but this reminder was necessary for understanding the meaning of the term *refusal of femininity*. To refuse one's femininity, for a neurotic, means to refuse fearfully the imaginary risk of losing some part of his being or losing his being entirely: "I don't want to submit or remain dependent on an Other whom I regard as an omnipotent father, one whom I believe to be capable of penetrating and destroying me, but whom I love nonetheless." Neurosis thus has four components: anxiety about feeling myself threatened by a perverse Other (a father); the stubborn refusal to open myself to him; the imperious demand that he continue to love me; and the effects of anxiety, namely the obliteration of thought and, through symptoms, the obliteration of the body. You can well imagine that in such a subjective state the neurotic will have a great deal of trouble assuming the role of a father. First because his own father, the father of his fantasies, is already occupying that whole space (the neurotic, in fantasy, remains a child), and then because he cannot and will not identify with that father whom he fears, loves, and detests.

In contrast, let's consider the man who accepts his feminine aspect. This man has succeeded in passing through the ordeal of anxiety and in understanding that, whatever the outcome of that passage, there remains an inevitable loss. Before this he had been anxious at the thought of risking his whole being; now he has come to understand that, despite the risks of this psychic ordeal, he will never be entirely destroyed and that in any event he will lose a part of himself. He no longer has to make a choice, but instead he has to live through what he must live through. In this successful passage, the Other of his fantasies stops being a castrating father and becomes simply one person among others, marked by a limit common to all human beings. This means that the subject who has passed beyond the ordeal will integrate his feminine part; he will calmly accept both the absence of a sexual identity established once and for all and the impossibility of defining precisely the nature of the male sexual being and the female sexual being. *Accepting his feminine aspect is, for a man, to agree to maintain his sexed being as an enigma that enlivens and animates his desire.* When a man who has thus admitted his femininity eventually becomes a father, he will be in the best subjective position to lead his children to the threshold of the ordeal that opens onto adulthood.

11

Hysterical Blindness in the Theories of Charcot, Janet, Freud, and Lacan

Let us now consider the conversion symptom that is universally acknowledged as emblematic of hysterical suffering, namely hysterical blindness. In a succinct paper, Freud (1910) uses this visual disturbance as an illustration of the psychoanalytic concept of symptom formation. He mentions the different theories of the etiology of hysteria proposed by the French school of the period (Charcot, Janet, Binet, etc.) and invites the reader to consult the works of these authors. Having followed Freud's advice and consulted various treatises of hysteria published in France at the end of the nineteenth century, I was astonished at the extreme similarity of views, particularly between Freud and Janet.

Indeed, in Janet's (1894) major work, *L'État Mentale des Hystériques*, we find remarkable passages and incisive formulations concerning hysterical blindness. Certain statements from this book and other works of Janet were taken up almost verbatim by Freud. Formulations that analysts have attributed to Freud are entirely the work of Janet, as, for example, the statement made by Freud in the 1910 paper and discussed in numerous analytic writings: "Hysterically blind people are only blind as far as consciousness is concerned; in their unconscious they see" (p. 212).

These affinities between Freud's work and that of the French school have prompted me to chart the developmental course of the theories of Charcot, Janet, and Freud on the origin of hysterical blindness. Starting with Charcot, the conceptualization of hysteria changes progressively up to the radical break made by Freud. For the sake of completeness, I have added a discussion of Jacques Lacan's contribution.

*

CHARCOT'S THEORY OF HYSTERICAL BLINDNESS

"I No Longer See" Equals "Blindness."

For Charcot (1888–1894), as for many other psychiatrists of his time, especially Briquet, hysteria is an illness caused by the decisive action of an idea or a psychic representation heavily invested with affect. If the representation is strong, that is, if it represents an intense, excessive feeling, then it will have the enormous power of transferring itself brutally into the reality of the body and appearing in the form of a somatic symptom. If, through hypnosis or autosuggestion, an idea enters the subject's permeable psyche and takes on a high affective valence, the body at once enacts the content of the idea. The representation of a movement that is strongly felt—"I feel that I am walking"—is already the movement on the way to being executed, and the subject actually walks. In the opposite case, the representation of the absence of movement—"I can't walk anymore"—we have motor paralysis. In short, for authors such as Briquet, Charcot, and Bernheim, hysterical physical suffering is the result of the plastic embodiment of an idea, or, more precisely, of the translation into the language of the body of a grammatical sentence, whether affirmative or negative. (The grammatical nature of the sentence must be emphasized, since it is on just this point that Janet came into conflict with his master Charcot.) We can easily infer that hysterical visual disturbance, in which the subject can potentially lose his sight, is due to the impact of a strongly charged representation that, as it were, says: "I can no longer see."

Charcot and Bernheim hold this view in common, but the two masters of psychiatry differ on most questions concerning hysteria. One of the most marked divergences is the following. Charcot believes that the pathogenic representation is introduced into the subject during a traumatic incident caused by an external agent. By way of evidence, he demonstrates that a command issued to a hypnotized subject can bring on a hysterical symptom. For Bernheim, on the other hand, the representation arises spontaneously in the subject via autosuggestion; the hysteric who tells himself that he cannot see automatically becomes blind.

*

JANET'S THEORY OF HYSTERICAL BLINDNESS

> For Janet, Charcot's "I no longer see" is replaced by a "seeing" that wanders in the subconscious and is equivalent to the absence of seeing in consciousness, that is, to blindness.

A student of Charcot and a contemporary of Freud, Pierre Janet devoted many works of great rigor to the phenomenon of hysterical blindness. Like all other authors of this period, he based his theory (1894, 1895) on the principle, set forth by Charcot and Briquet, that an idea overly charged with affect will inevitably effect a somatic alteration. Hysteria, according to this view, is an illness that comes about through representation.

While largely accepting this theory, Janet introduced a number of corrections, some of which are of great importance for us, the psychoanalysts of today, because they were taken up by Freud and then transmitted to us by several generations of analysts. Janet postulates the necessity of distinguishing two radically different levels in psychic life. Following the theory—which I find extremely interesting—of Maine de Biran, and, even earlier, Leibniz, he differentiates between the conscious and subconscious levels, both of which are contained in a more global agency that Janet calls the ego.* This ego is able to synthesize, in a single perception called the *personal perception*, the two registers, conscious and subconscious. For example, the subconscious perception "seeing" is immediately felt by my consciousness to be a sensation that belongs to me, and the ego effects a perception that synthesizes both aspects in the form "I see."

It is in this context that Janet develops his etiological theory of hysteria. He hypothesizes that the illness is caused by the inability of the ego to synthesize a feeling and the thought that grasps it, an affect and the words that express it. In the absence of the synthesis, the ego becomes split, and the distance between conscious and subconscious increases to the point where there are two completely autonomous agencies. What happens in the case of hysterical blindness is as follows.

Translator's note: The French term here is *le moi,* "the me." In response to my query, Dr. Nasio noted that Janet's term *subconscious* refers to what Freud would later call the *unconscious*.

For Janet the psychic representation "I no longer see," which Charcot had held to be the origin of blindness, is too complex to be recognized and integrated by the weak ego of the hysteric. Instead of Charcot's over-permeable ego that allows the representation "I no longer see" to enter the psyche and become converted directly into blindness, Janet suggests that the hysterical ego is too weak to elaborate the affect "seeing" by means of a coherent thought. Because it cannot synthesize a complex phrase like Charcot's "I no longer see," the most abstract components of this phrase, the personal pronoun "I" and the negation "no longer," are suppressed, and what is retained is only the simple subconscious sensation of "seeing." As a primitive element, a pure sensation, this "seeing" escapes any influence of a weak synthesizing ego that might elaborate it into a unit comprising an agent, the "I," of an abstract process, the negation. Charcot's "I no longer see" is located in an indefinite mental domain, Janet's "seeing" in the highly determinate realm of the subconscious. Janet calls such a representation a fixed subconscious idea, refractory to the hysterical ego.

The representation "seeing" thus remains highly charged with affect, isolated, detached from the ego, at large in the space of the subconscious. Because it is excluded from and unintegrated with the set of representations constituting the hysterical ego, visual activity will also be missing among the other ego functions. To put it another way, since the ego lacks the representation "seeing," the subject will lack sight. Hysterical blindness, then, is brought about not by the *action* of a representation, as with Charcot's "I no longer see," but by the ego's *lack* of the subconscious representation "seeing."

Considered in the light of Freud's trauma theory of hysteria, Janet's "fixed idea" is clearly the twin of the Freudian irreconcilable representation. These appear to be identical twins, but, as happens with twins, they become entirely different once sexuality erupts onto the scene. For it is here that Freud's revolution begins. If Janet was no Freud, it is precisely because he was unaware that the affect investing the fixed idea is sexual affect.

*

FREUD'S THEORY OF HYSTERICAL BLINDNESS

> *Janet's subconscious "seeing" is replaced, in Freudian theory, by unconsciously "seeing" the genitals. Blindness is the result of a violent repression exercised by the ego against a perverse unconscious: "Since you're so eager to see sexual things, well, now you won't see anything at all anymore."*

Freud keeps Janet's theory of the unconscious and the dissociation within the ego, but he introduces the revolutionary factor of sexuality: unconscious "seeing" is a feeling of scoptophilic sexual pleasure obtained from the sight of the love object's sexual appeal. I want to emphasize that sexuality has a double aspect. It is to be found both in the pleasure of looking (scoptophilia) and in the object that is looked at (sexual appeal). Once we consider "seeing" to be a sexual feeling and the object looked at to be a sexual object, the entire dynamic of the relation among ego, consciousness, and the unconscious changes and must be completely revised.

Since the unconscious "seeing" is sexual, the hysterical ego does not, as Janet had thought, try to assimilate and synthesize the "seeing"; on the contrary, it tries to isolate it still further and, in a word, to repress it. For Janet the hysterical ego is ill because it is weak, while for Freud, as we shall see, it is ill because it is too easily offended. The ego represses the "seeing," the sexual representation that it finds intolerable, so violently that it abolishes any visual functioning whatsoever. Hysterical blindness, according to Freud, is the self-injurious result of excessive repression carried out by an ego struggling against unbearable sexual "seeing."

If we compare Freud's theory of the psychogenesis of a conversion symptom with the two theories of the French school, therefore, we have three quite distinct conceptions of the hysterical ego: too permeable, too weak, or too desperate.

*

A READING OF LACAN'S THEORY
OF HYSTERICAL BLINDNESS

> *Unconsciously "seeing" the genitals in Freud's theory becomes, for Lacan, "the ego is an erogenous eye that looks at the genitals of the Other," and this becomes "the ego is a phallus that looks at the phallus of the Other," which, finally, becomes "the ego is a phallus that looks at the power/impotence of the Other."*

I shall not repeat here the exhaustive study of Lacan's theory of the gaze that I have presented elsewhere (Nasio 1986–1987). I shall simply note what I consider to be his essential contribution to the Freudian theory of hysterical blindness, his advance over the three preceding theories. His substantial modification of the Freudian account of hysterical blindness can be summed up by saying that he fantasmatizes it. Lacan interprets "unconsciously 'seeing' the genitals" as an action carried out between two protagonists in a fantasmatic scene, the ego and the other. "Seeing" the genitals in the unconscious thus becomes "the ego sees the genitals of the Other." These two characters, the ego and the Other, are the actors in the castration fantasy. On the one side we have the ego, no longer the repressing ego described by Freud but an erogenous ego-eye that visually seizes upon the flaw of the castrated Other. Opposite this ego we have this Other, a characteristic figure who, having been castrated, has no genital except the hole left by the absence of the phallus. Thus "'seeing' the genitals in the unconscious" becomes "erogenous eyes looking at the Other's hole." If we follow the logic of the castration fantasy that I have set forth in previous chapters, we can say that the erogenous eye-ego not only perceives the flaw in the Other but identifies with the phallus-object of which the Other is deprived. It then follows that the ego-phallus visually perceives the Other's lack of a phallus. In more general terms, we may conclude that the ego is itself a sexual organ in search of the flaw in the Other, whether this flaw be impotence or excessive potency.

In the hysteric's eyes, then, the Other's genital is neither the penis nor the vagina but his flaw as revealed by too much weakness or too much power. What moves a hysteric is not sexual charm (in the sense of the genital) but the charm that derives from the strength or, on the contrary, the fragility of the partner. Freud states that the hysteric's blind eye sees nothing consciously, but unconsciously sees the beloved other's erotic charm. For Lacan, I would suggest, the hysteric's blind eye is seduced by the erotic charm that emanates from another person who is neither virile nor feminine, but rather faulty or omnipotent.

12

Excerpts from the Works of
Freud and Lacan on Hysteria*

The cause of hysteria is not the trauma of an aggression from with-out, but the psychic trace left by the aggression. It is this trace, over-loaded with affect, isolated, painful for the ego, that is at the origin of the hysterical symptom.

"The psychical trauma—or more precisely the meaning of the trauma—acts like a foreign body which long after its entry must continue to be regarded as an agent that is still at work" (Breuer and Freud 1893, p. 6).

*

The origin of hysteria is the trace of a trauma with sexual content.

"At the bottom of every case of hysteria there are *one or more occurrences of premature sexual experience*" (Freud 1896, p. 203, emphasis in original).

---

*The comments in italics preceding each selection are those of the author.

*

Hysteria is an illness brought about by an inefficient ego defense, repression. Hysteria is therefore called "defense hysteria."

"The outbreak of hysteria may almost invariably be traced to a *psychical conflict* arising through an incompatible idea setting in action a *defence* on the part of the ego and calling up a demand for repression" (Freud 1896, pp. 210–211, emphasis in original).

"[I]n order to form a hysterical symptom a defensive effort against a distressing idea must be present" (Freud 1896, p. 213).

*

Conversion is a failure of repression. It consists in the transformation of an energic overload that passes from a psychic state (an irreconcilable representation) to a somatic state (bodily suffering).

"In hysteria the incompatible idea is rendered innocuous by its *sum of excitation* being *transformed into something somatic*. For this I should like to propose the name of *conversion*" (Freud 1894, p. 49, emphasis in original).

*

Excerpts from three major authorities on hysteria, showing that conversion symptoms do not obey the laws of anatomy or physiology but instead depend on another, distinctly imaginary, anatomy.

Janet: "These [hysterical] anesthesias in geometrical segments correspond not to anatomical regions innervated by a spinal column, but to entire organs as imagined and delimited in popular thinking. They take the form of a jacket sleeve, a leg of lamb, a wristband" (1894, vol. I, p. 111).

Freud: "I . . . assert that the lesion in hysterical paralyses must be completely independent of the anatomy of the nervous system, since *in its paralyses and other manifestations hysteria behaves as though anatomy did not exist or as though it had no knowledge of it.* . . . [Hysteria] takes the organs in the ordinary, popular sense of the names they bear: the leg is the leg as far up as its insertion into the hip, the arm is the upper limb as it is visible under the clothing" (1893, p. 169, emphasis in original).

Lacan: "[N]either paralysis nor anesthesia occurs according to the pathways and topography of the nerve branches. Nothing in neural anatomy corresponds to anything whatsoever that occurs in hysterical symptoms. It's always a question of an imaginary anatomy" (1955–1956, p. 201).

*

The suffering experienced by a hysteric in a conversion symptom is equivalent to orgasmic satisfaction, and the part of the body that is the site of the conversion takes on the value of a sexual organ.

"[T]he patient's symptoms constitute his sexual activity" (Freud 1906 [1905], p. 278).

*

The conversion symptom disappears if it assumes a symbolic value produced by the analyst's listening.

"[T]he clearing up of the symptoms is achieved by looking for their psychical significance" (Freud 1905a [1901], p. 41).

*

Freud changes his theory of the etiology of hysteria: the cause of hysteria is no longer a trauma but a fantasy.

"[T]he 'traumatic' element in the sexual experiences of child-hood lost its importance. . . . It was only after the introduction of [the] element of hysterical phantasies that the texture of the neurosis and its relationship to the patient's life became intelligible . . ." (Freud 1906 [1905], p. 274).

"Hysterical symptoms are nothing other than unconscious phantasies brought into view by 'conversion'" (Freud 1908, p. 162).

*

The sexual life of the hysteric is a paradox that causes suffering: a highly erotized body coexists with an anesthetized genital area.

"[T]he enigmatic contradiction which hysteria presents [is] the pair of opposites by which it is characterised—exaggerated sexual craving and excessive aversion to sexuality" (Freud 1905b, p. 165).

"I should without question consider a person hysterical in whom an occasion for sexual excitement elicited feelings that were preponderantly or exclusively unpleasurable; and I should do so whether or no the person were capable of producing somatic symptoms" (Freud 1905a [1901], p. 28).

*

What is disgust? It is a violent rejection of genital sexuality, carried out not on the genital level (vaginismus, etc.) but on the digestive level. The mouth becomes a genital that vomits, and the sexual partner is reduced to a repulsive object.

"It is in the function in which the sexual object moves towards the side of reality and presents itself as a parcel of meat that there emerges that form of desexualization that is so obvious that it is called in the case of the hysteric a reaction of disgust. . . . It was no accident that I chose the function of disgust. There are really two major aspects of desire as it may emerge in the fall of sexualization—on the one hand, disgust produced by the reduction of the sexual partner to a function of reality, whatever it may be, and, on the other hand, what I have called, in relation to the scopic function, *invidia*, envy. Envy is not the same thing as the scopic drive, nor is disgust the same thing as the oral drive" (Lacan 1964, pp. 172–173).

*

For Lacan, the hysteric's desire is above all a desire for dissatisfaction. This idea is also to be found in Freud.

"If what hysterics long for the most intensely in their phantasies is presented to them in reality, they none the less flee from it, and they abandon themselves to their phantasies the most readily where they need no longer fear to see them realized" (Freud 1905a [1901], p. 110).

*

The hysteric adopts, with astonishing ease, the role of both the man and the woman, but especially that of the third party who generates the conflict. He stages dramas, gets mixed up in conflicts, and then, once the curtain has fallen, he becomes aware, in the pain of solitude, that everything was merely a game from which he has been excluded.

"Identification is a highly important factor in the mechanism of hysterical symptoms. It enables patients to express in their symptoms not only their own experiences but those of a large num-

ber of other people; it enables them, as it were, to suffer on be-
half of a whole crowd of people and to act all the parts in a play
single-handed" (Freud 1900, p. 149).

*

*Lacan has summed up in a difficult but remarkable formulation the
power of the hysteric to extend outwards—well beyond the limits
of our real body—the intense presence of the libidinal body. The
libido here is an organ that, like a flexible and extensible arm, can
carry very far the libidinal body that Lacan calls "the being of the
organism."*

"The libido is that thin plate that slides the being of the organism to its true limit, which goes further than the limit of the body.
This plate is an organ of being, an instrument of the organism;
it is sometimes sensitive, as it were, when the hysteric plays at
testing its elasticity to the utmost" (Lacan 1966, p. 848).

*

*The hysterical woman does not know what the feminine genital is,
and in order to find out she passes through the intermediation of
the father, the bearer of the penis. The hysteric takes up her abode
in the father's desire in order to know, from that place, what it is
that a woman has that is desirable, and in order to try to feel what
her father feels in possessing a penis. In this way she believes she
will perhaps succeed in symbolizing the female sexual organ.*

"When Dora finds herself wondering, *What is a woman?*, she is
attempting to symbolize the female organ as such. Her identification with the man, bearer of the penis, is for her on this occasion a means of approaching this definition that escapes her. She
literally uses the penis as an imaginary instrument for apprehend-

ing what she hasn't succeeded in symbolizing" (Lacan 1955–1956, p. 178).

"What is it to be a woman? and specifically, *What is a feminine organ?* Notice that here we find ourselves before something odd—the [hysterical] woman wonders about what it is to be a woman, just as the [hysterical] male subject wonders about what it is to be a woman" (Lacan 1955–1956, p. 172; emphasis in original).

"The desire of the hysteric [is] to sustain the father's desire" (Lacan 1964, p. 50, translation modified).

References

Abraham, K. (1924/1953). A short study of the development of the libido, viewed in the light of mental disorders. In *Selected Papers, Volume I,* trans. D. Bryan and A. Strachey, pp. 418–501. New York: Basic Books.

Audouard, X. (1984). *La Non-Psychanalyse ou l'Ouverture.* Paris: L'Étincelle.

Benoit, P. (1985). Le saut du psychique au somatique. In *Psychiatrie Française* 5:85–97.

Breuer, J., and Freud, S. (1893). On the psychical mechanism of hysterical phenomena: preliminary communication. *Standard Edition* 2:3–17.

Charcot, J.-M. (1888–1894). *Oeuvres Complètes.* Paris: Bureaux du Progrès Médical.

Colloquium (1988). *Fin d'un analyse, finalité de la psychanalyse.* Colloquium held at the Sorbonne, May 1987. Mouvement du Coût Freudien, Solin.

Ferenczi, S. (1924/1968). *Thalassa. A Theory of Genitality,* trans. H. A. Bunker. New York: Norton.

Freud, S. (1893). Some points for a comparative study of organic and hysterical motor paralyses. *Standard Edition* 1:157–172.

——— (1894). The neuro-psychoses of defense. *Standard Edition* 3:43–61.

——— (1896). The aetiology of hysteria. *Standard Edition* 3:189–221.

——— (1900). *The Interpretation of Dreams*. *Standard Edition* 4–5.

——— (1905a) [1901]. Fragment of an analysis of a case of hysteria. *Standard Edition* 7:3–122.

——— (1905b). *Three Essays on the Theory of Sexuality*. *Standard Edition* 7:125–243.

——— (1905c). Psychical (or mental) treatment. *Standard Edition* 7:281–302.

——— (1906) [1905]. My views on the part played by sexuality in the aetiology of the neuroses. *Standard Edition* 7:270–279.

——— (1908). Hysterical phantasies and their relation to bisexuality. *Standard Edition* 9:157–166.

——— (1909). Some general remarks on hysterical attacks. *Standard Edition* 9:229–240.

——— (1910). The psycho-analytic view of psychogenic disturbance of vision. *Standard Edition* 11:210–218.

——— (1915). Repression. *Standard Edition* 14:143–158.

——— (1917) [1915]. Mourning and melancholia. *Standard Edition* 14:239–258.

——— (1933). *New Introductory Lectures on Psycho-Analysis*. *Standard Edition* 22:3–182.

——— (1937). Analysis terminable and interminable. *Standard Edition* 23:216–253.

Freud, S., and Breuer, J. (1895). *Studies on Hysteria*. *Standard Edition* 2.

Gurewich, J. F., and Tort, M., in collaboration with S. Fairfield. (1997). *The Subject and the Self: Lacan and American Psychoanalysis*. Northvale, NJ: Jason Aronson.

Janet, P. (1894). *État Mentale des Hystériques*. Paris: Rueff et Cie.

——— (1895). Un cas d'hémianopsie hystérique. *Archives de Neurologie* 99:337–342.

Jones, E. (1913). *Papers on Psycho-Analysis*. New York: William Wood.

Lacan, J. (1955–1956). *The Seminar of Jacques Lacan. Book III: The Psychoses*, ed. J.-A. Miller, trans. R. Grigg. New York: Norton, 1993.

——— (1960–1961). *Le Séminaire. Livre VIII: Le Transfert dans sa Disparité Subjective*. Paris: Seuil, 1991.

——— (1962–1963). *Le Séminaire. Livre X: L'Angoisse*. Unpublished.

——— (1964). *The Four Fundamental Concepts of Psychoanalysis*, ed. J.-A. Miller, trans. A. Sheridan. New York: Norton, 1981.

——— (1966). *Écrits*. Paris: Seuil.

——— (1970–1971). *Le Séminaire. Livre XVIII*. Unpublished.

——— (1977a). *Écrits. A Selection*, trans. A. Sheridan. New York: Norton.

——— (1977b). Propos sur l'hystérie. *Quarto*, vol. 2, September 1981. (Belgian supplement to *Lettre Mensuelle de l'École de la Cause Freudienne*).

Laplanche, J. (1974). Panel on hysteria today. *International Journal of Psycho-Analysis* 55:459–468.

Maillet, C. (1988). Phobies. *Patio* 10, Éd. de l'Éclat.

Moebius, P.-J. (1888). Über den Begriff der Hysterie. *Centralblatt für Nervenheilkunde* 2:66–71.

Nasio, J.-D. (1985). L'inconscient, le transfert et l'interprétation du psychanalyste: une vue lacanienne. *Psychanalyse à l'Université* 10(37):87–96.

——— (1986–1987). *Le Regard en Psychanalyse*, I and II. Unpublished seminar.

——— (1987). *Les Yeux de Laure. Le Concept d'Objet a dans la Théorie de J. Lacan*. Paris: Aubier.

——— (1988). *Enseignement de 7 Concepts Cruciaux de la Psychanalyse*. Paris: Rivages.

——— (1989). *Leçons sur la Technique Psychanalytique*. Unpublished seminar.

——— (1990a). *La Guérison*. Unpublished seminar.

——— (1990b). Interview with N.-E. Thévenin. In *Futur Antérieur* 2:103–110.

——— (1990c). *L'Hysterie ou L'Enfant Magnifique de la Psychoanalyse*. Paris: Rivages.

Tarán, L. (1965). *Parmenides: A Text with Translation, Commentary, and Critical Essays*. Princeton: Princeton University Press.

ABOUT THE AUTHOR

Juan-David Nasio, psychiatrist and psychoanalyst, is Director of Studies at the University of Paris VII (Sorbonne) and Director of the Séminaires Psychanalytiques de Paris, a major center for psychoanalytic training and the dissemination of psychoanalytic thought to non-specialists. He is a former member of the École Freudienne of Jacques Lacan and worked closely with the renowned child analyst Françoise Dolto. He is the Editor of the Psychoanalysis Series at Éditions Payot.

The author of eight books on psychoanalysis, Dr. Nasio has published numerous articles and interviews in leading publications and has participated extensively in French radio and television broadcasts. He lives in Paris, where he practices psychoanalysis with adults and children.

Index

Printed in the United States
by Bookmasters

Printed in the United States
By Bookmasters